D1191197

Gift
8-99

THE CORNISH NIGHTMARE

(D. H. Lawrence in Cornwall)

by

C. J. Stevens

PR
6023
A93
292395
1996

John Wade, Publisher
Phillips, ME. 04966

The Cornish Nightmare

Copyright © 1996 by C. J. Stevens

All rights reserved.

No part of this book may be reproduced or transmitted in any form or by any means without the written permission of the author or publisher, except by a reviewer quoting brief passages. Address inquiries to John Wade, Publisher, P.O. Box 303, Phillips, Maine 04966.

Library of Congress Cataloging in Publication Data
Library of Congress # 96-61325

ISBN # 1-882425-06-5 (cloth)
ISBN # 1-882425-07-3 (paperback)

First Edition
Printed in the United States of America

Acknowledgments

Portions of the Stanley Hocking interview first appeared in *The D. H. Lawrence Review*, University of Arkansas Press, Volume 6, Number 3, Fall 1973.

The paragraphs accompanying the interview material are from my biography, *Lawrence at Tregerthen*, published by The Whitston Publishing Company in 1988.

Photograph acknowledgments are made to Barbara Weekley Barr, Evan Blandford, London Library, Mrs. Cecily Lambert Minchin, Library of University of Nottingham, Kitty Rogers, Studio St. Ives, Thames and Hudson Archives, and Thomson Newspapers, Ltd.

I thank the Hocking family for providing the cover photograph of D. H. Lawrence's phoenix. The tapestry was given to them shortly after the Cornish episode.

I address this book to Stella Stevens—
wife, love of my life, and grammatical watchdog.

Contents

Illustrations

The Cornish Nightmare

INTRODUCTION

D. H. Lawrence, the father of the modern love novel, has been documented in hundreds of memoirs and full-scaled portraits, but there is one period that has never been explained fully. This is the span of nineteen months during World War I, from March 1916 to October 1917, when Lawrence and his German wife, Frieda, lived in a small cottage by the sea in Cornwall and were suspected of spying for the German submarine crews operating off the Cornish coast.

The war coincided at a crucial time in Lawrence's life. His marriage was in trouble, he was uncertain of his sexual preferences, and he was tormented by the long lists of casualties from the front and the mass patriotism around him. It was the end of the old world for him, and he reacted by going back to the land and by forming an intense relationship with William Henry Hocking, a handsome Cornish farmer who lived nearby.

I met Hocking's younger brother, Stanley, the "Arthur" of Lawrence's *Kangaroo*, while searching for the records of my paternal ancestors in St. Ives, Cornwall, England during the winter of 1967-1968. Two of my forefathers had lived near Tregerthen, in Zennor, during the eighteenth century. Someone suggested that I see Stanley Hocking. His family had been tenants on Tregerthen farm for several generations.

As I expected, Mr. Hocking was unable to help me or suggest where I might look for further information. But I found that he had an astonishing memory, and I was much impressed with his ability to present incidents from his past. He made life on Tregerthen farm very real for me. When a second cup of tea was offered by Mrs. Hocking, I accepted gratefully. Hocking told me that he had given up Tregerthen in 1962 when he retired and moved to St.

Ives. "It was a good life," he said, and then pausing, added: "I find it easier to remember things that happened more than fifty years ago than to recall things that went on last week!" And what did he consider to be the most interesting time in his life? "I've had many," he replied, "but I'm sure it would be the time when D. H. Lawrence and his wife, Frieda, were with us."

I was a very inquisitive visitor for the next hour and a half. My host barely had time to answer one question before I interrupted with another. I could see that my curiosity pleased him, and he was in no hurry to change the subject. Near the end of our long talk he asked his wife to fetch his Lawrence clippings and some needlework, explaining to me that he had difficulties at times with his legs—particularly when "negotiating" a staircase.

Mrs. Hocking returned with a metal box filled with yellowing newspaper clippings, and what appeared to be a glass-framed picture. Hocking rose stiffly from his chair. "This is a little keepsake that Lawrence gave our family," he said. It was a tapestry of the phoenix on its nest of flames. "Lawrence made this," Hocking explained. "He was very often busy with a needle." Then Hocking showed me his clippings and a school composition book in which he had written "a few notes" about Lawrence and Frieda. His material lacked organization, but the little he had recorded had been presented interestingly. He had a definite feeling for words, and I told him this. He was happy to have my confidence in a matter which obviously plagued him, though he waved my opinion aside, pausing to say: "I don't suppose I shall ever get it all down." We talked about other things for a few minutes, and Lawrence wasn't brought up again until I was at the door thanking the Hockings for a very enjoyable afternoon. "Our little chat has brought to mind several items about Lawrence that I had forgotten," he declared as I left.

It was more than a month before I saw Hocking again. I had just come out of a St. Ives shop as he was passing by. "You know," he said, "I've been thinking more and more about Lawrence since you dropped in." I told him that I was delighted to hear this, and expressed interest in our getting together again soon. He replied that he would be pleased if we did. "It's a pity I didn't have my tape recorder with me that day I came to see you," I said. The thought of recording our conversation didn't trouble him, but he expressed some concern as to how his voice would sound coming from a machine. After being assured that he would be agreeably surprised, he looked at me and said: "Look here, lad, why don't we get together and see how our next little talk sounds on your recorder?"

I had a bottle of port and the machine waiting when Hocking arrived at our cottage. For more than two hours I posed questions and he answered them. In the beginning of the interview he was aware of the recorder, and his responses were somewhat guarded. But the wine and the informal atmosphere of the surroundings soon relaxed him. Occasionally, he would break away from what he was saying to relate an entirely new piece of evidence. I listened and watched him. His speech rhythms seemed to erase the years for him, and he was back on Tregerthen farm and Lawrence lived nearby. At times, when held in a sort of trance by his own words, his reactions were those of a sixteen-year-old farm boy. I shall never forget his fascinating reply when I asked him if Lawrence liked Cornwall. "Of course he did. He could do what he wanted. He could go swimming at Wicca Pool, he could walk to St. Ives, he could take a ride in Tom Berryman's cart"—the enviable position of being an adult, as seen by a boy who must spend all day in the harvest field.

The tape had run out, the bottle of port was empty, and the interview was obviously over. But we both sat on: he, lost in a world he had known so well; I, the curious observer, sorry to have that world end so soon. "What are you going to do with it?" Hocking asked. For a moment I didn't understand him, and then the significance of his question became clear to me. I told him that I wanted to publish the interview. "It will be more than I have done, he said with a sigh. "You have my permission to do what you like with it."

I made a transcript of the interview the following week while my family and I were visiting in London, and I combed the city for books on Lawrence. I was disappointed to find that little had been written about Lawrence's farm friends. His letters to fellow writers about his literary activities at Higher Tregerthen were faithfully recorded—so much so that I began to doubt Stanley Hocking. How could Lawrence be so prolific as a writer and become so involved with his literary associates and still find time for the Hockings? A closer look at the letters that Lawrence wrote in Cornwall and a reading of "The Nightmare" chapter of *Kangaroo* which recalls that time with the farm family went far to restore my confidence. What Stanley Hocking had done was to give me a rare glimpse of Lawrence: a stranger who came into the hayfield "to be like them"—someone who enjoyed sitting by the old Cornish slab; a man who was completely at ease with them.

I met Hocking down by the St. Ives docks shortly after my return from London. I asked him if it would be possible for us to visit again, and he declared that it "would indeed be very possible." We made arrangements to meet over the same refreshments at my cottage.

He was in fine form throughout that next interview—relaxed and amusing. I found myself questioning him closely several times during the long session, particularly when his enthusiasm for the days gone by led me to think that he was exaggerating. Hocking usually had a reasonable explanation at hand, and when one was not available immediately he competently produced some new pieces of information to satisfy my curiosity. There was the risk that Lawrence was more than lifelike in his mind—I could see this as a danger during our first long talk—but Hocking had a sharp eye for detail and a genuine desire to get at some truth about Lawrence.

I had recorded several reels of tape before I saw the first hints of spring in St. Ives and on the Zennor footpaths. My time in Cornwall was coming to an end. When the weather turned sunny and warm Stanley Hocking and I spent several hours one day at Tregerthen farm and Higher Tregerthen. Evan and Doreen Blandford of Studio St. Ives accompanied us with photographic equipment, and Stanley Hocking pointed out the various settings where the many dramas took place. "I can see Lawrence crossing that little field now," said Hocking. "It seems only yesterday that he and Frieda were with us—it all happened fifty years ago."

"It was 1915 the old world ended," Lawrence wrote in "The Nightmare" chapter of *Kangaroo*. "In the winter of 1915-1916 the spirit of the old London collapsed; the city, in some way perished, perished from being a heart of the world, and became a vortex of broken passions, lusts, hopes, fears and horrors." During the early months of the war, Lawrence began to lose faith in his country. For him, the integrity of England was missing and he longed to escape the misery around him. He had planned to go to America, to Florida, but when the opportunity came he could not seem to break away; he and Frieda would find temporary shelter in the West Country of England. "We go next week," he wrote Lady Cynthia Asquith.[1] "Some members of our Florida expedition are coming down too—we begin the new life in Cornwall. It is real...."

Higher Tregerthen

HIGHER TREGERTHEN

Q: Do you recall just how the Lawrences happened to take one of the three cottages at Higher Tregerthen?

HOCKING: I was working in one of the footpath fields, not far from our old farmhouse, when Lawrence and Frieda came along. At first sight, they seemed to be a rather odd-looking pair, if you will. Lawrence had a ginger-colored beard, and he was dressed in a brown corduroy suit. He was wearing a slouch hat. Frieda was a very good-looking lady, fair and blonde, and above all things, she was wearing bright-red stockings. They said good evening very nicely and stopped to chat. They asked me if I lived at the farm. I told them that I was born there, and my grandfather and his grandfather before him. "Oh yes, that's interesting," Lawrence said. "We like this part of the world, and we think it would be an awfully nice place to stay. We'd like to live somewhere near here." He said they were staying at the Tinners Arms, in Zennor, but it would be for only a week or two. "Do you know of any vacant cottages around here?" Lawrence asked. "Oh yes, those cottages over there are all vacant at this moment," I told him. They were Higher Tregerthen. "They look rather nice," Lawrence said. "Do you think I could get hold of one?" I told him the name of the owner, and if he wanted to go and see him there wouldn't be any harm done. The owner was Captain Short, an old sea captain who lived in St. Ives. "Good," said Lawrence, "I'll see him tomorrow."

Q: This was early March?

HOCKING: Early March, 1916. A few days afterwards Lawrence

15

and Frieda called at the farm. Mother and I were there. They told us that they had succeeded in renting a cottage at Higher Treger-then for five pounds a year. Mind you, it was only a small cottage and unfurnished. Lawrence said they were going to get a few sticks of furniture together and go there to live. He said they hoped that they could get their few necessities of life from the farm. Mother said they could. So within a few days they got some secondhand furniture in St. Ives and moved into the cottage.

Q: Your farm was between Lawrence's cottage and the sea?

HOCKING: Oh yes, certainly. His cottage was only a few hundred yards from the farm. Just across one of our little Cornish fields. There had been various people of dubious character who lived at Higher Tregerthen during my school days. I suppose they were married, but they never stayed long. They were people of the laboring type, people who would work out somewhere and come back to the cottage to sleep.

Q: Were the cottages at Higher Tregerthen ever occupied by writers or artists prior to Lawrence's stay?

HOCKING: Yes. A man called Ranger Gull—you may know him as Guy Thorne.[2] Gull said he was going to live in the tower cottage, but he didn't. He had the bloody door of the tower painted with black and white stripes. I remember that.

Q: I understand Lawrence did his own carpentry while settling in at Higher Tregerthen?

HOCKING: Lawrence could turn his hand to anything. I remember seeing a dresser he made, and I can still see the walls he painted. Pale pink walls and the cupboards bright blue. He could cook too. He was a bit effeminate, and he did some embroidery work.

16

There were a few of his paintings on odd scraps of paper pinned up near the scullery, but I don't think Lawrence or Frieda attached any importance to them. They were very roughly done, hanging with several little bits of his crochet work. To use an old Cornish saying: "He could wash, mend, make and sew"—a saying of my mother's.

Q: Do you remember John Middleton Murry[3] and Katherine Mansfield?[4]

HOCKING: Very plainly. They were taking the tower part at Higher Tregerthen. They wanted to live next to the Lawrences, but only stayed for a very short time. It wasn't to their liking. The Murrys were always complaining that the place was wild, cold, and uninhabited, and they didn't like the roughness of the countryside. So they packed up and went to live on the Falmouth side of the coast.

Q: I understand that Murry and Lawrence quarreled?

HOCKING: Yes. I think that was the real reason why the Murrys left Zennor. They didn't like the area, and they found reason to quarrel with Lawrence.

Q: Katherine Mansfield claimed that Lawrence beat Frieda up, and that Frieda went running to Murry for him to save her.

HOCKING: I don't believe it. What date was this piece of information written?

Q: On the spot, I believe. In a letter from Katherine Mansfield to S. S. Koteliansky.[5] And I assume this letter was made public after Lawrence's death.

17

HOCKING: Of course. Dead men can't hear and they don't bite. They wouldn't have dared to print that if Lawrence had been living. And I don't believe for one moment that this is true.

Q: Most of Lawrence's friends and biographers agree that the Lawrences did quarrel, and that sometimes these quarrels were quite violent.

HOCKING: I can hardly believe it. They had their little tiffs, but I don't think they quarreled as violently as that.

Q: Catherine Carswell[6] has stated that in 1916 Frieda more than once thought that Lawrence was going mad.

HOCKING: I can definitely say that Lawrence was never mad. I think people wrote things about the Lawrences because it made sensational reading. One thing they didn't do: they didn't write things while Lawrence was alive. If he was mad, we would have known. After all, he was with us for two whole summers and one winter.

Q: Do you recall the time Frieda hit Lawrence over the head with a stone plate and nearly brained him?

HOCKING: No. But I believe Catherine Carswell mentioned this little incident in her book on Lawrence. When Frieda read it she was pretty mad. I saw it in a magazine, or one of our weekly Sunday papers. Frieda made a very vigorous denial to Catherine Carswell's statement.

Katherine Mansfield, in her letter to S. S. Koteliansky, on May 11, 1916, explained that she hadn't written earlier because everything had been so unsettled. She was being left alone too much at

Higher Tregerthen. It wasn't a nice place. "It may all be over next month; in fact, it will be. I don't belong to anybody here." Mansfield reported that she and Frieda weren't speaking to each other. The rift had developed because Katherine couldn't tolerate the situation between Lawrence and Frieda. "I don't know which disgusts me worse. When they are very loving and playing with each other or when they are roaring at each other and he is pulling out Frieda's hair and saying 'I'll cut your bloody throat, you bitch' and Frieda is running up and down the road screaming for 'Jack' (Murry) to save her."

Middleton Murry recalled an evening when he and Katherine Mansfield were sitting by the fire in the long room of the tower cottage when suddenly a shriek. Frieda rushed in crying: "He'll kill me!" Lawrence followed, pale and in a frenzy. He chased Frieda several times around a table, shouting: "I'll kill her, I'll kill her!" Chairs were overturned, and Murry barely managed to save a lamp. "Katherine sat still in a corner, indifferent, inexpressibly weary." Murry wrote in *Between Two Worlds*: "I was terrified. That he would have killed her, I made no doubt; and yet, for some strange reason, I had no impulse to intervene." Then suddenly Lawrence dropped into a chair by the fire, his fury spent. They were all silent. Frieda went back to their cottage. "The three of us sat on without stirring—each in our different way, utterly exhausted. After a time, Lawrence rose, pale and shaky, and said good night." The episode was over. But what bewildered both Murrys even more than this outburst was what they found when they visited the Lawrences the next morning. The two were "sitting side by side, to all appearance blissfully happy, while Lawrence trimmed a hat for Frieda."

The table-chasing row was only one of many eruptions at Higher Tregerthen, and according to Murry, these usually came about from some ordinary occurrence. Frieda would contradict Lawrence and he would explode. Murry remembered one recurring argument. Frieda would "defend one of Lawrence's discarded prophets—Shelley, for example, or Nietzsche—"and she would be too sweet and reasonable." Lawrence would attack. "What do you know about Shelley, I'll—," then a threat and his air of righteous indignation. Murry claimed that Frieda knew the lie of the land concerning Lawrence's sympathies at any given moment. But still she persisted in holding her own, and against him.

Recalling this time in Cornwall, Frieda remembered "days of complete harmony between the Murrys and us. Katherine coming to our cottage so thrilled at my foxgloves, tall in the small window seat. Since then whenever I see foxgloves I must think of Katherine." And Frieda and Katherine would frequently walk to Zennor village with Katherine Mansfield stamping her feet at the high wind she hated so much, and later the two would sit talking like "two Indian braves." Then one day they all went out on the sea in a boat, and Frieda was moved when they sang "Row, row, row your boat/Gently down the stream"—Frieda finding something "strangely significant" in the words, and Lawrence's rage because "I was so bad at keeping my part of the song going."

Brigit Patmore,[7] who first met Lawrence and Frieda in London during World War I, felt that the quarrels were never serious. Patmore suggested that the rows were aggravated by the presence of Lawrence's literary friends. But once caught in the cross fire of crockery and pots, or witnessing one of Lawrence's verbal whippings, friends found it difficult to take such performances lightly or to think of the quarrels as being therapeutic. Just under the surface an unalterable bond did exist, and perhaps it was this that kept the Lawrences together to the end.

Mabel Dodge Luhan,[8] who knew the Lawrences in New Mexico, gave her readers this picture of Frieda: "I saw the big voluptuous woman standing naked in the dim stone room where we dressed and undressed, and there were often great black and blue bruises on her blond flesh." Then one morning Luhan found Frieda in tears. When asked what was wrong, Frieda cried: "He tears me to pieces. Last night he was so loving and so tender with me, and this morning he hates me." Such a statement came as no surprise to Mabel Luhan. She and others had been present when Lawrence shouted at his wife: "You sniffing bitch, stop your smoking." And when Frieda asked why she should, Lawrence was enraged. "Take that dirty cigarette out of your mouth! And stop sticking out that fat belly of yours!" But Frieda wasn't defeated easily; she was quick to counterattack. "You better stop that talk or I'll tell about your things." Lawrence jumped to his feet and swung at her head. She ducked and ran from the room. The onlookers were shocked, and their discomfiture became astonishment when they saw Lawrence and Frieda a few minutes later walking in the moonlight, arm in arm like lovers.

"I do think a woman must yield some sort of precedence to a man," Lawrence wrote Katherine Mansfield in 1918. "I can't help it, I believe this. Frieda doesn't. Hence our fight." And once when confronting Frieda, Lawrence pressed her against a wall with his hands on her throat and told her that he was her master. Frieda's reply that he could be her master as much as he liked, that it made no difference to her, surprised him so that he dropped his hands. A fight to the death was how Lawrence saw marriage, and Frieda's opposition to his wish for dominance led them close to the breaking point on more than one occasion. When really stung by his unreasonableness, she could resist with all her stout stubbornness. Their brawls were sometimes hideously petty; sometimes grand. She would rile him by smoking too much, eating too many cakes, having her hair cropped, and taking an opposite line of thought. Frieda once complained to Edward Garnett[8] that Lawrence "always wants to treat women like the chicken we had the other day, take its guts out and pluck its feathers sitting over a pail."

Catherine Carswell's *The Savage Pilgrimage*, largely a personal narrative, revealed Lawrence as a man of immense energy, quick to fly into rages over the smallest things, and courageous. A hero who repudiated heroism. And Frieda was to Lawrence "a buffeting and a laughing breeze, a healing rain or a maddening tempest of stupidity, a cheering sun or a stroke of indiscriminating lightning." Much of Carswell's book was a fence-mending reply to Murry's *Son of Woman*, but both she and Murry produced similar versions when reporting the continuous rows at Higher Tregerthen.

More than once in 1916, Frieda felt that her husband was mad. An incident in which she nearly brained him with a stone dinner plate showed that both were unpredictable. Lawrence was washing dishes in the scullery and singing a roundelay—he and Frieda had just concluded a bitter argument. Frieda came in from the living room carrying the stone dinner plate. The song Lawrence was singing "so wrought upon her," Carswell wrote, "that her wrath boiled afresh. Down on the singer's head she brought the dinner plate." It could have injured Lawrence seriously. "But he was so far from bearing a grudge as from turning the other cheek. 'That was like a woman!' said he, turning on her viciously, but on this occasion too much astonished to strike back. 'No man could have done such a thing when the quarrel was over, and from behind too!' Then Lawrence added: 'But you *are* a woman.'"

Louis Untermeyer,[9] who first met the Lawrences in Italy and later in London, found Frieda "an almost theatrical contrast to her husband." Her solidness and good health made her "the earth-mother Lawrence was always seeking and escaping, but to which he always returned." Frieda took pride in her role and her family and she was quick to let one know that she was a von Richthofen and her husband was only a commoner. She wouldn't be pitied for the difficult days she and Lawrence shared in Cornwall "when she lived," wrote Untermeyer, "servantless and unfriended, in a flimsy shack on the coast of England." She never did the menial chores about the house. That was her spouse's task. "Lawrence scrubbed the floors. He loved it."

Emma Maria Frieda Johanna von Richthofen was born in 1879, the second of three daughters of Baron and Baronin Friedrich von Richthofen. Her father had begun his career in the military, though

22

later he served as an official in the civil service. Frieda grew up outside Metz and knew the Germany of Bismarck and the Kaiser's court. In 1898 the wild, high-spirited girl met the Englishman, Ernest Weekley,[10] whom Aldous Huxley labeled "possibly the dullest professor in the western hemisphere," and much to the surprise of everyone who knew Frieda, she married the etymologist and went to live in the industrial setting of Nottingham where Weekley had been appointed a university lecturer. She had three children, a boy and two girls, a splendid home, and an automobile for her own use. But Frieda was bored and even her love affairs had little meaning for her. Lawrence was twenty-seven years old—Frieda, thirty-four and married twelve years—when he came to see his former professor about a teaching recommendation. Frieda may have been ready to give up her husband, but leaving her children was a torturous decision to make. There was no denying it: Lawrence woke what had been asleep in her for so long—a need for excitement and a renewed appetite for life.

But living with a different man didn't end her affairs. Frieda was amoral, sexually. Her unfaithfulness to Lawrence was frequent throughout their married life; even when they were first living together she made love to a woodcutter she didn't know, as David Garnett[11] recalled, "just to show Lawrence she was free to do what she liked." Sexual relations with Lawrence's friends, such as Middleton Murry, Cecil Gray,[12] and Harold Hobson,[13] and with Italian peasants, including Angelo Ravagli[14] who would become her third husband, were carried on without much discretion. Frieda was generous with her body. Yet she needed Lawrence and depended on him. He seemed more concerned about his own sexual life—particularly when she accused him of being impotent. Frieda's sexual ethics shocked her daughter, Barbara Weekley, at the time of Lawrence's death. Not only did Frieda share her bed with Murry and refuse to end her long affair with Ravagli, but according to Lawrence scholar Emile Delavenay,[15] Frieda repeatedly locked her daughter in a bedroom with the Calabrian youth who

23

had made the phoenix for Lawrence's grave at Vence. She felt it would cure Barbara of "the fits of delirium and violent outbursts of hatred against her mother." Two years before his death, when Frieda returned home after seeing Angelo Ravagli again, Lawrence, who well knew what was going on, said to her: "Every heart has a right to its own secrets."

Frieda resented having to live in the shadow of Lawrence's mother, Lydia Lawrence. His attachment to his mother left him incapable of forming a normal relationship with other women. Lydia always intervened. He expected all women to dress the way she did, to cook like her, and when he scrubbed floors he did them the way she had taught him. Her codes of propriety were his—the only explanation for the fact that the author of *Lady Chatterley's Lover* believed that sexual intercourse was indecent at any time except in the middle of the night. His many domestic accomplishments—Stanley Hocking's old Cornish saying of being able to "wash, mend, make and sew"—were learned in childhood to please his mother and to be useful to her.

Lawrence's mother, the young Lydia Beardsall, was impressed with Arthur Lawrence's black beard and his accomplishments on the dance floor. He made his work in the coal mines sound romantic, and his rustic ways and speech amused her. She had been a schoolmistress, had written verses, and had been jilted by a refined young man when the coal miner entered her life. They were happy together in the beginning of their marriage, but Arthur Lawrence broke his pledge and began stopping for beers with his friends at the pubs on his way home from work at night. She nagged and scolded him and the scenes turned ugly. There were children now, and the love she had felt for her husband was lavished on her offspring and against him. As Lawrence wrote when developing *Sons and Lovers*: "But as her sons grew up she selects them as lovers—first the eldest, then the second. These sons are *urged* into life by their reciprocal love of their mother—urged on and on. But when they come to manhood, they can't love, because their mother is the strongest power in their lives, and holds them." Lawrence wanted to fill the void in his mother's life by returning her love but such an undertaking was too much. It left him incapable of accepting a woman's love and with a fear of women.

If Lawrence's mother hadn't died of cancer at the age of fifty-eight, in 1910, and had she lived another twenty years, surviving Lawrence who died in 1930, she probably would have overpowered him. Yet her death didn't free him. He tried to escape when killing her symbolically in the writing of *Sons and Lovers*, by administering an overdose of medicine to mercifully end her suffering, but the ties were too tangled and deeply knotted. Frieda had to put up with his mother's death from the first, and after the symbolic killing to a lesser degree, but the loss was always there to come between them. Frieda didn't suppress her irritation. In a notebook where Lawrence kept his poems, she once penned a message suggesting that he should go back to his mother's apron strings. And another time she wrote a skit called "Paul Morel, or His Mother's Darling." Lawrence read it, and in a frosty voice declared: "This kind of thing isn't called a skit."

Diana Trilling,[16] in her introduction to *Selected Letters of D. H. Lawrence*, wrote that it was the combination of the war and his marriage that brought Lawrence close to the breakdown. He never should have institutionalized the relationship. Live with Frieda, yes. But once his sexual feelings for his wife became a "social regularity and conventional family emotion, it brought sex into the established connection with love." Trilling suggested that Lawrence wanted Frieda to love him like a mother, but after the couple were married, Frieda became "the very mother person from whom she had supposed to detach him." Trilling felt that Lawrence needed "a German woman like Frieda to stay entirely sane and make a successful career of the lunacy" of their marriage.

Frieda was hopelessly clumsy when faced with practical matters. The telephone was too difficult for her, and she was unable to do the simplest household chores with any competence. Even when using words, though she was sensitive to them, she was never able to express herself adequately. This led people to think of her as being stupid and trivial. She was exceedingly tactless, and as Diana Trilling assessed her: "a bit of a swamp, she had a swampy mind and spirit." Frieda was indolent, careless in her dress, and inclined to put on weight. Cecily Lambert Minchin,[17] who knew the Lawrences after Cornwall, recalls: "I can see her now on that evening, sitting back on a low arm chair, purring away like a lazy cat and shewing a great deal of plump leg above the knee encased in calico bloomers probably made by D. H. himself. She was not permitted to wear silk or dainties."

Frieda must have felt lonely from time to time throughout their marriage. Many of Lawrence's friends were hostile to her, and the demands her husband placed on her to fit his conception of their union must have eroded some of Frieda's good humor. Lawrence had been known to rudely dismiss the few friends she made on her own. She rarely was able to see her children while they were growing up, and they were told by their father, Ernest Weekley, that their mother wasn't a worthy person and was best forgotten. Then there was the death of her father, in addition to the many relations and childhood acquaintances who were dying at the front in the German forces.

Lawrence's puritanism surfaced frequently. He may have sewed Frieda's calico bloomers himself, but he snarled at her for sitting with her legs apart. It was he who insisted that they get married for decency's sake. It is sometimes difficult to think of Lawrence as the apostle of our sexual revolution; the writer who wanted to make sex beautiful and not an act of shame; all this from a man who was an outright sexist. One never knew where Lawrence stood—he would recoil at the sight of exposed flesh and he would write about the sexual act with a boldness that shocked critics into charging him with pornography. He wasn't one who appreciated smutty stories. Lawrence disliked them intensely—the way his mother no doubt did—and he showed his displeasure whenever he heard them. But he didn't object to rank words being used to ornament or clarify sentences. Frieda's enjoyment in taking whatever came her way with amoral gluttony often caused his black moods to soar. She was the opposite of his mother in all her thoughts and actions.

Lawrence beat Frieda, he treated her shabbily before strangers and friends, but he was lost when she was away from him. She knew that much of his irritability came from illness, and she guarded his health valiantly while he continued to abuse her. Sometimes the gentle side of his nature astonished her—she once bumped her head against a shutter and he showed concern and sympathy. But he would soon turn on her again and they would argue bitterly.

"I am no Jesus that lies on his mother's lap," Lawrence wrote Baronin von Richthofen. "Oh mother-in-law, you understand as my mother finally understood, that a man doesn't want, doesn't ask for love from his wife; but for strength, strength, strength. To fight, to fight, and to fight again." This was written years after the Cornish episode, in 1923, when the Lawrences had learned some ground rules for their feuding. In Cornwall, a sickness overcame Lawrence. The most desperate battles of his marriage were fought at Higher Tregerthen.

Frieda von Richthofen

BLUTBRÜDERSCHAFT

Katherine Mansfield felt that Middleton Murry was too much under Lawrence's influence at Tregerthen, and she was determined to
break the spell. Her resistance to the friendship between the two
men caused Murry to back away from Lawrence and to grow closer
to Katherine. Then the demands of a *Blutbrüderschaft* became ur-
gent. Lawrence insisted there had to be a bond between them and
this could only be achieved by a sacrament performed on the dark
Cornish moors. Such a blood rite frightened Murry, and Lawrence
became more exasperated. Lawrence would turn against Frieda
after being with Murry. "If I love you, and you know I love you,
isn't that enough?" Murry asked his friend. And Lawrence pro-
claimed: "I hate your love, I *hate* it!" Then one night the Murrys
heard Lawrence shout to Frieda: "Jack is killing me!"

It was during this time that Lawrence was writing his novel
Women in Love. When Murry read it four years later and wrote a
hostile review of it, he was unaware of being cast in the story.
Only when Frieda told him that he and Katherine were included
could he see that his and Lawrence's *blutbruder* conversations
approximated those between the novel's characters Gerald Crich
and Rupert Birkin. And he was Crich, Frieda pointed out. "Any-
how," Murry wrote, "that was a rough way of putting it; I was not
Gerald Crich, but it probably is true that Lawrence found the germ
of Gerald in me, as he found the germ of Gudrun in Katherine."

Lawrence felt that Murry's relationship with Katherine was dead-
ly. It didn't have the life-giving union that he had with Frieda.
But Lawrence needed a new relationship with Murry to complete
his marriage with Frieda. Rupert (Lawrence) tells Gerald (Murry):
"You've got to take down the love-and-marriage ideal from its ped-
estal. We want something broader. I believe in the *additional* per-

fect relationship between man and man—additional to marriage." Murry was convinced that his friend was undergoing a change at Tregerthen. Lawrence wasn't at all the unselfish man he had once known. "What he really wanted of me," Murry wrote, "he never put into words, and to this day I am doubtful whether he ever knew. But what he imagined he wanted is stated clearly in the novel."

Frieda Lawrence insisted that her husband was never homosexual, but later in life she admitted that Lawrence "did not disbelieve in homosexuality." She was convinced that he and Murry never had a "love affair." (Professor Emile Delavenay, author of *D. H. Lawrence and Edward Carpenter*, in a letter to me, C. J. Stevens, claimed that Frieda was very guarded in her remarks concerning all Cornish incidents at Higher Tregerthen and Tregerthen farm, that Frieda was busy creating the Lawrence legend as early as 1932, and that she was jealous of Lawrence and all his friends.)

The semi-homosexual tie Lawrence tried to establish with Murry came at the time that Lawrence was demanding complete submission from Frieda. They had to be concurrent. As early as 1913, he wrote: "I believe a man projects his own image on another man, like on a mirror. But from a woman he wants himself reborn, reconstructed. So he can always get satisfaction from a man, but it is the hardest thing in life to get one's soul and body satisfied from a woman, so that one is free from oneself." Lawrence was unsuccessful in both. Frieda wasn't about to conform to his expectations of submissiveness, and Murry was too unsettled by Katherine Mansfield's mood at Higher Tregerthen to pledge himself on the Cornish moors. Lawrence's inability to establish the relationship he wanted kindled his violent rages and brought him close to the breaking point.

Lawrence wanted a man friend all his life and never was the need greater than during the war years in Cornwall. The intense feelings he had for Murry were showered on William Henry Hocking when it became obvious that Katherine Mansfield had won in the struggle over Murry. Aside from the friendship with William Henry, visiting the Hockings was in many ways for Lawrence a return to the Haggs farm and the Chambers family—a farm only two miles from his boyhood home in Eastwood. "Bert" Lawrence loved the Chambers family, and he was often with them (as described in his novels, *The White Peacock* and *Sons and Lovers*), playing charades, carrying on high-spirited conversations, and helping in the fields with the harvest. "Work goes like fun when Bert's there," said Mr. Chambers. And Mrs. Chambers declared: "I should like to be next to Bert in heaven." Lawrence loved to be with the two Chambers boys, Alan and Hubert, and later with Jessie, the sensitive young girl who soon wanted more education after meeting the young Bert. In a letter to J. D. Chambers, youngest son of the Chambers family, written in November 1928, Lawrence looked back on those early days. "Whatever I forget, I shall never forget the Haggs—I loved it so. I loved to come to you all, it really was a new life began in me there." And Lawrence concluded: "If there is anything I can ever do for you, do tell me—Because whatever else I am, I am somewhere still the same Bert who rushed with such joy to the Haggs."

Lawrence's favorite was Alan Chambers, and he was with his farm friend often, working in the hayfield and helping with the chores. In his first novel, *The White Peacock*, 1911, Cyril, the Lawrence figure, declares that his friendship with George Saxton (Alan Chambers) was "more perfect than any love I have known since, either for man or woman." And in a discarded prologue to *Women in Love*, Lawrence is more explicit. His feelings are clearly expressed in Rupert Birkin's response: "All the time, he recognized that, although he was always drawn to women, feeling more at home with a woman than with a man, yet it was for men that he felt the hot, flushing roused attraction which a man is supposed to feel for the other sex."

He loved Alan Chambers, and the young farmer was fond of his friend, whose knowledge of the world impressed him. But illness,

31

and Lydia Lawrence's jealousy when she became aware of Jessie Chambers's interest in her son, kept Lawrence more and more away from the Haggs and his male companion. In *Sons and Lovers*, Paul Morel tells Miriam that if only she had been a man their relationship would have been ideal. The comment didn't go unnoticed by Miriam, who knew of his longing for a profound friendship with her elder brother. A parallel situation developed at Tregerthen. Frieda, the mother figure, was jealous of her Bert's intense interest, not in a Jessie this time, but in the new Alan Chambers—William Henry.

The handsome Tregerthen farmer wasn't characterized in *Women in Love*, but he is clearly brought to mind in the unused prologue: "There would come into a restaurant a strange Cornish type of man, with dark eyes like holes in his head, or like eyes of a rat, and with dark, fine, rather stiff hair, and full, heavy, softly-strong limbs. Then again Birkin would feel the desire spring up in him, the desire to know this man, to have him, as it were to eat him, to take the very substance of him. And watching the strange, rather furtive, rabbit-like way in which the strong, softly-built man ate, Birkin would feel the rousedness burning in his own breast, as if this were what he wanted, as if the satisfaction of his desire lay in the body of the young, strong man opposite." Fiction isn't reality, though this discarded section reads more like a prologue for men in love. But Lawrence did pack the pages of his fiction with clear and often cruel descriptions of people he met casually or knew well. The "Cornish type of man" Lawrence described is an accurate snapshot of William Henry, a true likeness which even catches a gesture or two of the man as he sits eating at the table.

"Was there really a thing between them?" Mabel Dodge Luhan claimed to have asked Frieda in 1922. And Frieda replied: "I think so. I was dreadfully unhappy." One can imagine the scene of seduction—perhaps somewhere in the darkness on the shaggy moors where the Druidical boulders suggest a blood ceremony. But it would be only speculation; no evidence has been unearthed to confirm such a culmination. And we can't expect a "stout-hearted" farmer to react in the same way as a well-educated and indecisive John Middleton Murry. Land and animals were Hocking's principal concerns. Out of nowhere, Lawrence appeared, and he understood Hocking's fear of death. Then the two talked of dying and the powers of death and the young farmer was wide awake to the wonders of the unknown. A curious selfishness kept their relationship alive as Lawrence spoke of bloodconsciousness—continuously probing—Hocking misunderstanding and intentionally misunderstanding. It would have been impossible for William Henry to accept all that was being suggested. Lawrence's *blutbruder* probes went far beyond William Henry's comprehension, but Hocking did little to discourage his friend. In fact, he coaxed Lawrence on, and both men felt renewed as Lawrence reiterated his ideas of blood sacrifice.

Catherine Carswell, in her *The Savage Pilgrimage*, wrote: "I have heard Lawrence say that sexual perversion was for him 'the sin against the Holy Ghost,' the hopeless sin." Lawrence assured Carswell that his relationship with Hocking was "no sin against the Holy Ghost." He often expressed his aversion to homosexuality— sometimes so vehemently that one wonders why all the commotion, as when he wrote Koteliansky in 1915: "We have had another influx of visitors: David Garnett and Francis Birrell[24] turned up the other day—Saturday. I like David, but Birrell I have come to detest. These horrible little frowsty people, men lovers of men, they give me such a sense of corruption, almost putrescence, that I dream of beetles."

For Katherine Mansfield, another problem at Higher Tregerthen was Lawrence's obsession with sexual symbolism and man's animal nature. She was unable to see phallic comparisons in trees, brooks, and pen fillers. Mansfield suggested to Lawrence that he should call his cottage "The Phallus" and Frieda was quick to agree. It is interesting to note how the name "John Thomas" appears and reappears in Lawrence's fiction: William Henry Hocking was characterized as "John Thomas Buryan of Trendrinnan farm" in "The Nightmare" chapter of *Kangaroo*; it was used for the tram conductor in the short story "Tickets Please"; and the second draft of *Lady Chatterley's Lover* was originally called *John Thomas and Lady Jane*. "John Thomas," Lawrence wrote Mabel Luhan, "is one of the names for the penis, as you probably know."

REALITIES

Q: You spoke of Frieda wearing red stockings. Was she eccentric in her choice of clothing?

HOCKING: Oh no! She always dressed very nicely. I saw her once or twice in a Bavarian costume which was attractive. I think her hat was red and white with a wide brim. Whether or not it was the Nelson style hat, I can't remember. But her dress and bodice were very picturesque—a sort of laced-up affair in front with a black skirt and a tiny little apron, worked with flowers.

Q: Lawrence once wrote that Frieda loved music. He said that nothing would keep her indoors when she heard a trumpet.

HOCKING: That could be. They had a piano in the cottage, and she used to play it a bit. It was an old one, but it sounded rather well. I must admit my accordion would not harmonize with Frieda's playing at all.

Q: When she spoke did she have a trace of an accent?

HOCKING: Frieda spoke fairly good English, though I could detect what I would call an accent when she pronounced certain words. Do you recall that song, "Row, row your boat?" Well Frieda could sing it very nicely, but she would always sing: "Woe, woe your boat."

Q: Whenever I think of Lawrence I get a picture of a man of average height, perhaps a bit on the tall side, thin, with a rust-colored beard, and for me, he's always dressed in either tweed or corduroy.

HOCKING: You've got a good picture of him. He frequently wore a corduroy suit. But when he went to St. Ives, I remember he had a decent gray suit. When he was at home, or came into the fields to help us, he would dress in anything. Old shoes. Old trousers. An old hat. He said he wanted to look like one of us.

Q: Tell me, Mr. Hocking, if you crept up behind Lawrence and *suddenly* put your hand on his shoulder, how do you think he would respond?

HOCKING: Oh my! Oh gosh! That would be the wrong thing to do with Lawrence! I wouldn't like to do that. He would probably take it as an insult. He wasn't one who was going to be manhandled by anyone. If Frieda found fault with him about anything, he would immediately fly into a rage. Lawrence had a quick temper, I must admit, and didn't like to be criticized.

Q: Did he ever tell you people his reason for wearing a beard?

HOCKING: Yes. And his reason was quite simple: to keep his throat warm. He frequently suffered from bronchitis.

Q: Was Lawrence a man of many moods?

HOCKING: Yes. At times, Lawrence was quite lighthearted and could see fun in anything. Then on other days he would be depressed, as if something was worrying him. What that was we never knew.

Q: It has been said that Lawrence was homosexual.

HOCKING: Certainly not. Not to my knowledge. I refuse to believe that Lawrence was homosexual. No, no! He already had a woman to dapple with.

Q: I read in Lawrence's *Kangaroo* that your local postman was also a Wesleyan preacher. I understand he was too old for the military, but he enjoyed handing out those On His Majesty's Service envelopes which summoned a man for military service.

HOCKING: Yes. I remember him, and he's long since dead. But I'm not going to tell you his name. He came from a well-known St. Ives family.

Q: Lawrence wrote that this man "had a religious zest added to his natural Cornish zest" of enjoying "other people's disasters." That the "thought of hell for other men was sweet in him."

HOCKING: I'm not sure his zest was *Cornish*, but it is a very good way of putting it.

Q: I'm wondering if the postman ever saw any of the German newspapers he was delivering to the Lawrences?

HOCKING: I wouldn't know about that.

Q: Did Lawrence ever argue with the man?

HOCKING: My word! No! I think there was a certain hostility between the two, and Lawrence felt a bit uncomfortable when the man was at the door, but the postman and Lawrence shied away from each other. The postman would give a grin when he came with those wretched envelopes. I knew the attitude. He was our postman for many many years.

Upon receiving his summons, Lawrence reported to the military authorities in Penzance for his physical examination, and Frieda rode over the moors with him in Tom Berryman's wagon. Much to Lawrence's surprise, he was ordered to proceed to Bodmin, in central Cornwall. He said good-bye to Frieda, and Berryman drove her back to the lonely cottage at Higher Tregerthen. On the sixty-mile train trip to Bodmin the other recruits sang all the patriotic and sentimental songs of a nation at war. They were lined up on the station platform and marched through the streets to the barracks. Lawrence felt the camaraderie of the men was a degradation. It was losing one's individuality and becoming part of the mob spirit. He liked the men who went with him, though he believed they had made a mistake by choosing to serve—answering the colors when called was one thing but enlisting was another. They were all brave men, yet not one was capable of rejecting suffering. They were too willing to accept their miseries without demanding happiness, and Lawrence thought this a loss of integrity. They must stand by their fellowmen and be slaughtered. It was all too depressing for him. "This is what Christ's weeping over Jerusalem has brought us to, a whole Jerusalem offering itself to the Cross," he wrote Catherine Carswell. "This is the most terrible madness." At all cost, he wouldn't serve. Lawrence was keenly aware of how different he looked—a man with a beard. He sensed his isolation, and his beard became a symbol. If it had to be taken off, he would be defeated; it represented his independent manhood.

They all slept that night in Bodmin. The barracks seemed like a prison to Lawrence and he was reminded of Oscar Wilde in Reading Gaol. The food was bad but the sergeant was likable. Lawrence was ashamed of the patches on his underwear—he was so poor. He slept badly that night, kept awake by one man's cough and the groans of some men in their sleep. At dawn came the rush to the icy baths, the revolting breakfast, and the order to tidy the barracks. Lawrence was called "Dad" because of his beard. Then the physical examination. He stood while the doctors probed and asked their questions. Lawrence wasn't strong, and the doctors declared him unfit. But he was told to find some form of volunteer service. He kept silent, knowing this he wouldn't do. The other men looked at him resentfully because they thought he had been favored—he wasn't a working man. Lawrence had won his reprieve; for a time he would be safe; he was free. He hurried back to Higher Tregerthen to relate his experience to an anxious Frieda. They were both jubilant.

HOCKING: He came down to the farm and told us how he had been treated. "A ghastly experience," he said. "Most degrading to have to hop to and fro, stark naked in a room before a half dozen doctors." Lawrence didn't like that. He wasn't passed very high in his first examination at Bodmin, and the second time was rejected as unfit for military service. Lawrence said to me, after coming back from his first examination: "They will never make a soldier out of me."

Q: He was determined not to go?

HOCKING: He said he hated the whole thing. "I don't want to go and fight and kill anybody. And if the Germans come here and want my little cottage, they can have it. I wouldn't kill them."

Q: I understand that you people on the farm shared Lawrence's feeling. That you loathed the idea of being compelled to serve.

HOCKING: Well yes. Compulsion is never appealing to the Cornish. I don't think anybody wanted to go. The war was so far away, and as soon as anyone left a farm the whole way of life was disrupted. On a farm there are certain jobs to be done. If you have cattle, sheep, horses and pigs, they must be fed and looked after every day. And when one person from the family is missing, who is going to do his work? It's either trying to replace that person with someone else, which would be rather impossible, or making all the others do a lot extra.

Q: How did your brother William Henry stand with the military?

HOCKING: William Henry got an exemption right away. All tenant farmers and important men on our English farms were exempt from military service in those days, even if they were of age, providing they remained in their occupations. If they left the farm, they were immediately called up.

Q: Did Lawrence complain much about his health?

HOCKING: He wouldn't say anything about his health. The only thing he would admit to was that he had a bad cold occasionally.

Q: Richard Aldington[18] claimed that Lawrence was so ill with consumption that he was exempted from military service immediately.

HOCKING: I've heard of Richard Aldington. But I don't think he ever came to Tregerthen. Therefore, he wouldn't really know what his health was like during those two years that he was with us. Lawrence's health may have deteriorated quite a bit after he left us in October 1917, but I can say that he certainly showed no signs of consumption; perhaps an occasional touch of bronchitis, or a nasty cold or two that left him indisposed for a few days, but there was never much wrong with him.

Q: What did Lawrence tell you about his writing?

HOCKING: He never told me much about his writing. The only clue I got of publishers refusing his work was through Frieda, and she mentioned it quite often to me. She thought his writings were too much philosophy. Lawrence could always find something to write about, but the trouble with him was that he couldn't dispose of his work. He couldn't make any money out of it. I do know that he wrote some articles for the *English Review.*

Q: Do you recall just what those articles were?

HOCKING: Yes. They were called "The Reality of Peace." He gave us one or two copies of these, and he was rather pleased that they had been accepted. I believe Lawrence was writing a lot of articles in those days. They were nearly all returned as not quite good enough for publication, and when they did come back, they were very often burned. I was there one day when Frieda threw a bunch of them on the fire and burned them in front of him.

Q: She threw them on the fire?

HOCKING: Oh, yes. She told him off. I remember her saying: "There you are, Lorenzo, they've all come back again! Your writings are all philosophy and bosh and nobody wants them!" And into the fire they went. What they were I never knew.

Q: What did Lawrence do?

HOCKING: Lawrence got wild. He was very annoyed at this. I do remember him saying: "Never mind, some day I'll write something that will sell."

Q: Catherine Carswell claimed that Lawrence once almost set the chimney on fire at Higher Tregerthen while he was burning manuscripts.

HOCKING: I wouldn't be surprised. He had so many returned

that he probably wanted to get rid of them.

Q: Did Lawrence give you people any copies of his books while he was at Higher Tregerthen?

HOCKING: No, and he never said anything about his books to me.

Q: He had written several books by the time he came to Higher Tregerthen. Lawrence's *Amores* collection of poems was published in 1916, and he must have been preparing his *Look! We Have Come Through!* poems, for this collection came out shortly after he left Cornwall in 1917.

HOCKING: Did it? I wouldn't know about that. He talked a bit about poetry, but of course I haven't remembered what he said about it. I do remember him telling me that he was rather keen on making poems himself. And he quoted a few of Shelley's verses to me one day down by Wicca Pool.

Q: Do you recall how Lawrence happened to quote Shelley?

HOCKING: Yes, I can tell you the incident. It was a day in August. In fact, it was August 1917, just before he went away. I remember this distinctly. Wicca Pool was down by the cliffs where Lawrence and Frieda went swimming. They went there quite often during the summer months of June, July and August. Sometimes Lawrence would go there alone. I had been to see if the young cattle and sheep were all right on this particular day in August when Lawrence came along. He remarked on what a beautiful day it was. The sun was shining very brilliantly, without a cloud in the sky, and the sea was very blue. He said to me: "If we look about us, Stanley, here are all the things that Shelley wrote in his poem about the ocean. Do you happen to know the poem?" I said: "I'm afraid I don't know any of Shelley's poems at the moment." Then Lawrence asked if I would like to hear him recite a few verses. I said: "Yes, go ahead if you like." So Lawrence recited several verses to me.

Q: Have you read Lawrence's poetry?

HOCKING: I must admit I haven't seen many of his poems. I remember once telling two or three rather keen university students of an incident that occurred at the spring while Lawrence was at Tregerthen, and they thought it was what gave Lawrence the inspiration to write that poem about the snake. Do you know it?

Q: It's one of my favorites. What happened?

HOCKING: Well, in those days there was no water laid on at Higher Tregerthen. One had to go to the little spring, about a hundred yards up the hillside above Lawrence's cottage. There was a beaten path to the spring, and Lawrence used to go up there nearly every day with his pail. One day Lawrence told me that he had had quite an experience while going for his water. I asked him what it could be, since there was little between his cottage and the spring. He told me there was an adder coiled up and lying in the path. He said he stopped to look at her, and his first impulse was to kill her. "But on second thought," he said, "could I kill her? Oh no! She looked so beautiful there. Then as I approached," he said, "she raised her head and looked at me and slid away into the grass with the grace and poise of a beautiful princess!"

Q: Lawrence told you this?

HOCKING: Yes. I had to laugh. We don't admire adders that much. I remember my mother telling me that when she was a little girl of twelve and going to school, one of her schoolmates was bitten by an adder, and before they could get any medical help the child died. When I told Lawrence this, he didn't say any more about the snake. But it's rather an unusual thing to find: an adder coiled up in your path and basking in the sun. You don't see that very often.

This incident at the spring touched Lawrence deeply, and in his "The Reality of Peace" essays his experience of coming upon the adder began to take form: "If there is a serpent of secret and shameful desire in my soul, let me not beat it out of my consciousness with sticks." It would dwell in his subconscious where he couldn't touch it. "In its own being it has beauty and reality. Even my horror is a tribute to its reality. And I must admit the genuineness of my horror, accept it, and not exclude it from my understanding." Who is man to judge what must be on earth, and under the earth? Lawrence wondered. "I must make my peace with the serpent of abhorrence that is within me." And the snake must take its place with honor. "Come then, brindled abhorrent one, you have your own being and your own righteousness, yes, and your own desirable beauty."

But this wasn't the culmination. The final achievement had to wait until 1920, in Taormina, Sicily, when Lawrence recalled the adder at the spring at Tregerthen and wrote the best known of all his poems, "Snake."

Lawrence had gone for water—the scene: "On the day of Sicilian July, with Etna smoking." The princess had now become a "king in exile, uncrowned in the underworld," and voices in Lawrence said: "If you were a man/You would take a stick and break him now, and finish him off." But Lawrence confessed that he liked the snake and felt honored "That he should seek my hospitality/ From out the dark door of the secret earth." But as the venomous snake slowly drew up to ease himself "into/that horrid black hole," Lawrence picked up a log and threw it and the snake "writhed like

44

lightning, and was gone"—leaving Lawrence to regret his act. "And so, I missed my chance with one of the lords/Of life/And I have something to expiate;/A pettiness."

Q: Did you meet Robert Mountsier[19] and Esther Andrews[20] when they visited Lawrence?

HOCKING: Oh yes, the Americans who stayed in the tower part for the little time they were there. The two were at the Christmas party we all had.

Q: Do you recall the party?

HOCKING: Very clearly. This is getting on to the end of 1916. Lawrence, Frieda, Robert Mountsier and Miss Andrews invited William Henry, my two sisters, Mabel and Mary, and me up to the tower for the Christmas night party which they were going to give and wanted us to join in. So we went. That was quite interesting. Quite interesting. We all sat at a round table to begin with, Lawrence saying: "Everyone here shall be equal tonight." In addition to the ordinary Christmas fare, Frieda produced a dish she called "hot tamales." To me, they tasted like a superior sort of mincemeat, highly flavored with different spices, and served on a bay leaf. It was very nice. After supper we all sat around and sang different songs, and Frieda sang her German folk songs. In those days I could play an accordion. When Lawrence invited me to come up, he said: "Don't forget to bring your accordion, Stanley." So I did. I played, and they sang, and as time went on, I had exhausted myself in playing all my simple little tunes. I ran short. Lawrence said: "Can't you play just one more, Stanley?" I told him that I had played all that I could remember. Then I thought and said: "Yes, I can play just one more." It was the "Merrie Widow Waltz." Sad to say, Lawrence's face immediately fell. He said to me: "Please don't play that, Stanley! I really cannot stand it!" And I said: "Why, what's the matter, Mr. Lawrence?" "Oh," he said, "that reminds me of days gone by, and people gone by, and everything that's sad." And then he added: "Your instrument snorts like a prehistoric monster!"

Q: In the "Nightmare" chapter of *Kangaroo*, Lawrence wrote that a police sergeant called to check on Mountsier's papers and to question him. Was this mentioned?

HOCKING: Yes, it was brought up. Lawrence said: "We had a visitor last night. The police sergeant from St. Ives. He wanted to know all the details about us, including Mr. Mountsier." Lawrence said that Mountsier had told the policeman all he knew, and the man thanked him and went away satisfied. I knew that officer very well.

Q: Nothing more was said about this incident?

HOCKING: No. We were so engrossed in our little Christmas party. We were singing and joking, and nothing more was made of that particular affair. But that police sergeant came back afterwards with a military officer. I think it was the military who were really suspicious of the Lawrences.

Q: Perhaps you can clear up a little matter which puzzles me. In a letter to Barbara Low[21] on September 1, 1916, about six months after he moved into the Higher Tregerthen cottage, Lawrence wrote: "I wondered why you were so cross over Wm Hy. It is true, I still run away from him—and *cannot* ask him to the house. But he was talking to me on Sunday, and sighing for London, to see the searchlights etc. And I realized, with rather a shock, they truly hate him, all the rest. I thought they only *thought* they hated him. So I imagined if he had a few days in London it might help

46

him through the winter, especially if he had a few *people* in mind."

HOCKING: I don't understand any of this.

Q: Lawrence went on to write: "I wish one didn't always find a petty tragedy on one's doorstep—it wasn't that I wouldn't let you see him, here—it was that one *does* avoid him, he *is* rather a burden. He has never been inside the house yet, and for some reason, I cannot invite him. Perhaps it is best to ignore them as much as possible." Can you recall any reason why Lawrence should write this about your brother?

HOCKING: During the second year of Lawrence's stay at Tregerthen, my brother and he were jolly good friends. This is all very strange to me. Maybe Lawrence was a bit cautious when he first came to Tregerthen, but we soon consoled him.

Q: When Lawrence characterized your brother as "John Thomas" in *Kangaroo*, he wrote of your brother as being "his dearest friend" at the time.

HOCKING: They certainly were very friendly. Lawrence thought William Henry was more intelligent than the ordinary Cornish farmer. I know they liked to exchange views about everything.

Q: Lawrence wrote that your brother was always late.

HOCKING: I think William Henry had a bit of a record for that. The ostler in St. Ives often said: "Hocking's trap, always the last." Lawrence spoke about this the night when they gave us the Christmas party in the tower. My sisters and myself got to the party at the required time, but William Henry wasn't ready. He didn't go with us. And when we got up there we waited a full hour and still he hadn't come; I remember Lawrence saying: "That wretched William Henry, always late! Isn't he ever coming!" Eventually, he came and we all had supper together.

    The postmortem memoirs written by Lawrence's literary friends in the nineteen thirties, memoirs blaming the Cornish and the Hocking family for Lawrence's expulsion from the area, made lively reading. These reports were accepted and the obvious distortions weren't questioned. Scholars did visit Higher Treger-then to see the little cottage where Lawrence had lived, but few made the effort of questioning the local people who had known Lawrence. One visitor was unimpressed when a St. Ives resident offered to introduce him to William Henry Hocking. The man declined, yet he had come to Cornwall to gather new material. Lawrence's cottage depressed still another stranger, and he hurried-ly left Zennor, relieved that the pilgrimage was over.

    The Hocking family became increasingly reluctant to talk to strangers about Lawrence with the passing years. If William Henry had been approached differently before a lingering disease over-came him—probably Alzheimer's—perhaps some of the Cornish nightmare would have been brought into the open. Journalists should have asked William Henry how much hay he was cutting to the acre and how much manure was being plowed under for crops at Tregerthen before bringing up the subject of Lawrence. The few outsiders who did meet with the Hockings were only interested in D. H. Lawrence, the literary man, not the friend who came into the kitchen and sat talking by the old Cornish slab.

    The major interview with the Hockings was aired on November 14 and 22, 1953, with questions posed by Brenda Hamilton and Tony Soper of the Bristol branch of the BBC. The Hockings felt terribly uncomfortable throughout these two telediphone conversa-tions—they came across like barnyard folk, not overly alert but splashing plenty of local color. Stanley Hocking's ability to use words colorfully and his uncanny way of recalling incidents from the past were missing. William Henry was disoriented because of his illness, and the sisters, Mabel and Mary, were vague when answering questions.

Why were the Hockings and Lawrence so close? It had to be more than a return to the Haggs. And what kind of a person was William Henry? Was he truly an unreliable nonentity who failed Lawrence in the end? Biographer Harry T. Moore[22] suggested it, as did several of Lawrence's London friends.

"There was no one around that Lawrence could mix with," claimed Arthur Eddy, William Henry's uncle. "I suppose the two had things in common. "William Henry was very well liked, and he spent a lot of time reading. He had a lot of fun in him."

But Ivor Short, the son of the sea captain who rented Higher Tregerthen to Lawrence, said: "What kind of a person is a Cornish farmer? And there you are. William Henry was an ordinary Cornish farmer. He couldn't sit down and talk like we're talking. He could talk about farming. He could tell you about cattle and sheep, but when it came to discussing other things it was a different matter. Yet Lawrence and William Henry were great pals. I don't know how it came about."

"Oh, William Henry could talk. He could do that," said another uncle, P. O. Eddy. "That was the reason why they were such friends. Lawrence wouldn't have become friends with other farmers the way he did with William Henry. He was an influence in William Henry's life—to a certain extent. When my nephew found someone who could talk he would get all he could out of that person. I suppose this was what he did when he talked with Lawrence. William Henry was curious about things. If he had been living in this day and age, he would have had an education. But in those days there was no opportunity."

In a letter to Barbara Low, on 20 August 1916, after Low's visit to Higher Tregerthen, Frieda expressed concern for Lawrence's friend. "We are worried about William Henry, he is really interesting, we want him to have a 'lady' what would take an interest in

49

him—" Lawrence broke into the letter at this point with the plan of sharing the Tregerthen farmer with London friends. "I like Frieda's suddenly conspiring to marry off poor William Henry. He is desirous of the intellectual life, and yet he isn't in the least fit for anything but his farming. Perhaps during the winter I shall get him to go to London for a few days: then Dollie (Radford),[23] and you must look after him a bit." Lawrence felt there wasn't enough "mental continuity" to fling the Cornishman into the complexities of an intellectual life. It would require more than one generation for a man of such sensuous nature. "And he suffers *badly*, and his people hate him—because he *will* take the intellectual attitude, and they want only the vague sensuous non-critical." Lawrence believed his friend should break away from the family and live in one of the cottages next to him at Higher Tregerthen. "He looks to me as if I could suddenly give him wings—and it is a trouble and a nuisance."

One wonders how enthusiastic Lawrence's friends were when they learned that they must assume the responsibility of making William Henry's debut on the London scene a success. Lawrence was quick to tell them that he was involved because he felt sorry for the man. He wasn't ready to admit how friendly the two had become but the friendship was intense enough to convince Frieda that William Henry needed a woman.

"William Henry wants very much to come to London," Lawrence wrote Dollie Radford on September 5, "when harvest is over—next month, perhaps. Would you see him, and help look after him?" William Henry was filled with seeing the searchlights—he thought he could break away and make a visit. Lawrence doubted if his friend would move at all, knowing how slow William Henry was in getting in the harvest. "There is a great deal of friction down at the farm: the poor 'rascal and villain!' (Stanley and William Henry)—You knew that son-in-law, Hollow, was dead—three weeks ago. He went very rapidly. Mrs. Hocking is just beginning to cheer up a little." The son-in-law died of tuberculosis, and six years later his wife, Katie, next to the oldest of the four Hocking girls, died from the same disease. In addition to sickness and grief, Mrs. Hocking was being plagued by bickering in the household, often caused by William Henry's unusual ways of conducting farm business.

"I suppose there was some friction down at the farm," said Arthur Eddy. "I know William Henry's sisters and brother, Stanley, didn't appreciate him as much as they should have." The sisters found much to criticize in their eldest brother's irregular hours. His habit of beginning the farm day late in the morning was looked upon as laziness. "William Henry wouldn't start work the time the others did," P.O. Eddy recalled, "and then he would be working until long after dark. He never went to bed before midnight. He was an unusual Cornish farmer. Cornish farmers are very alert in the morning," explained Mr. Eddy. "They haven't a name for stopping in bed."

"Time didn't mean anything to Father," said William Henry's son, H. H. Hocking. "I remember we were working in the yard one day and it was dinnertime and I was starving. I said: 'Come on, Father, let's go in to dinner.' He stopped and looked at me and said: 'Let me tell you, Son, never put off until tomorrow what you can do today, and never put off till after dinner what you can do before.' This was the way he was. But Father was always late with one exception. To my knowledge, he was never late to a funeral. Everything else would have to wait when he paid his last respects to a person."

Lawrence was never able to see William Henry clearly as a person. He used the Cornishman as a symbol of Celtic perfection and declared his friend capable of intensities that he didn't exhibit. Lawrence came to Higher Tregerthen at a time when Hocking found life on the farm both dull and confining. The war was making demands on all farmers, and with so many men in uniform there were fewer laborers to help with the harvest. Lawrence's arrival on the scene did much to make life bearable for William Henry. He was also flattered that a man as worldly and educated as Lawrence should want him as a close friend.

"My father left school when he was thirteen," said H. H. Hocking. "He was in the top standard at school, but when a boy reached thirteen, he was expected to work. The teacher at the school in Zennor came to see my grandfather. The teacher wanted Father to become a teacher too. But my grandfather was a sick man, and since Father was the oldest of seven children, he was expected to go into what was then called 'The Service'—to go live with a neighboring farm family and do the odd jobs. Do the dirty work, I presume. My grandfather had only fourteen acres, and when he died, in 1901, there was three years of rent owing. Since Father was the oldest, he became the tenant. The owner told Father to carry on as best he could. Father paid back the three years' rent over a period of years, and in 1912, the landlord came to him and said: 'Look here, my lad, you've done your best and you can have some more land.' So from then on Father had the neighboring farm as well. He always said it was through the landlord that he ever got as far as he did."

"William Henry would always think that he had been done in," laughed P.O. Eddy. "I remember he once offered a cow to a man for thirty pounds, and the man said he would take her. Then William Henry was worried over the fact that he hadn't asked enough. I wouldn't have given twenty pounds for her. But that was William Henry for you. He did very well for himself."

A St. Ives resident, who insisted on remaining anonymous, felt that William Henry was a "tyrant" as a husband and when imposing discipline on his children. "A very difficult man." When asked about this side of his father's nature, H. H. Hocking paused and said: "I suppose Father was an unusual man. He was very strict with us children. My mother didn't have anything to say about naming us. What Father said would be it. But he was a kindly man and always very generous to beggars. The door at the farm would always be open to them, and they were never turned away.

They would be fed and put up in the barn to sleep, after promising not to start fires. Father was that sort of man, and I think Lawrence felt that he could come to the farm and sit down by the fire."

William Henry had a reputation of disrupting the peaceful Zennor setting with pranks. The Hocking family recalled some of the tricks he played on people. There was one memorable night when William Henry whitewashed all the windows of a farmhouse and the occupants were late in rising the next morning. "Father enjoyed a practical joke," said H. H. Hocking. "I remember hearing people tell about Father and his friends dropping clods of earth on the heads of people who were passing by the church fence in Zennor, and tying the wheels of the traps outside the Tinners Arms. The old men would come out of the pub and get into their traps and roar at their horses: 'Gee-up, gee-up!' But of course the traps wouldn't move—the wheels were tied. Father and his friends would be off in a dark corner, laughing."

Q: Did William Henry and Frieda get along? Lawrence wrote in *Kangaroo* that William Henry's greeting to her was sometimes like a jeer.

HOCKING: Oh, I wouldn't have thought that. They always got along very well.

Q: I believe your brother was one of several people Lawrence wanted to take with him on his Rananim scheme.

HOCKING: I did hear about that. Lawrence had an imaginary place which he was calling Rananim. He thought it would be a good idea if they went into another country and founded a little colony where they could all live happily ever after. Lawrence talked a lot about this. But I don't think anyone can live on imagination—you need something to eat and drink. But apparently this wasn't considered. And I think William Henry was thinking that the whole thing was nonsense, and he wasn't having anything to do with it. After all, you can't leave a farm. You can't pack up and leave your animals and relations and go somewhere to an imaginary place.

Q: Why do you think the idea of Rananim was so appealing to Lawrence?

HOCKING: Well, the war was going on then, and he very much wanted to go to America. He couldn't get there because the authorities wouldn't grant him permission. And Lawrence was also having difficulties in getting his writings published in this country. I remember him saying that he thought he would try getting them published in America.

Q: Tell me, were the Lawrences friendly with many people in Zennor?

HOCKING: No, they were only friendly with us Hockings. They didn't visit many people—only one or two. They knew Cecil Gray at Bosigran Castle house and Katie Berryman in Zennor village.

Q: Katie Berryman had the grocery store in Zennor, I believe.

HOCKING: That's right. The Lawrences used to get a few items at the grocery shop which was attached to the old post office in Zennor. Katie Berryman ran the shop, and her husband, Tom, had the post office. Katie and Frieda became quite friendly, and I do know that the Lawrences enjoyed the old lady's saffron cakes. They always said she was very nice to them.

Q: I understand Tom Berryman took the Lawrences around in his car?

HOCKING: Horse and trap; there were no cars around. Tom Berryman used to hire out in those days to drive people to town or to
the station. There were no buses then.

Q: Lawrence mentioned in one of his letters Meredith Starr[24] and
a Lady Mary[25] who lived nearby. If I recall, he wrote that Lady
Mary was the daughter of the Earl of Stamford. They were "herb-
eating occultists" so Lawrence pointed out. Do you remember
them?

HOCKING: I should think I do! Those two!

Q: In what way?

HOCKING: They were living in a little cottage at Treveal—about
a mile east of us. One night in St. Ives, while the old Pavilion was
still in existence at Porthminster Beach, those two put on a concert. Lawrence, Frieda, William Henry, myself, and I believe my
two sisters, Mabel and Mary, drove to see it in our usual horse and
rally cart. And of all the damn rubbish in the world it proved to
be! It was ridiculous! The two were hooted out before the concert
was over. It was certainly an amusing episode, and it got described in the local press.

Q: What happened?

HOCKING: They did the most senseless songs and dances you
ever saw. They brought in a rather well-known violinist here in
town, and he played some violin solos which were very highly
respected. But apart from that, it was all rubbish. Starr and Lady
Mary tried to put on the whole concert themselves. Lawrence was
very disgusted with it. "Had I known," he said, "I would have nev-

55

er gone to see it."

Q: Lawrence had several visitors while he was living at Higher Tregerthen, in addition to Mountsier, Miss Andrews, and the Murrys. Do you remember any of them?

HOCKING: I do recall Catherine Carswell and Barbara Low. But we weren't particularly interested in whom the Lawrences had for visitors. They would come down to the farm with Lawrence when he came for his drop of milk. Typical city people; people who lived in a different world. I never got into conversation with Barbara Low or Catherine Carswell. They were just introduced as friends of the Lawrences.

S. S. Koteliansky

Lawrence, Katherine Mansfield, Frieda, and John Middleton Murry, the day the Lawrences were married, July 13, 1914.

D. H. Lawrence

Katherine Mansfield and John Middleton Murry (1914)

William Henry Hocking

TREGERTHEN FARM

Q: I believe it was in Frieda Lawrence's book *Not I, But the Wind* where I read that when Lawrence came back from visiting you people at the farm he would frequently quarrel with Frieda.

HOCKING: Would he? Lawrence probably quarreled with her before he came down to see us. He used to come on numerous occasions, in addition to giving me my French lessons at the farmhouse table. I remember one particular night he came when we didn't really expect him. But Mother was rather wide awake when he came down on a rough night. I remember her saying to me before I had the lesson: "They had a row this evening. That's why he's here." It was a wild and stormy night. In the midst of my lesson, an occasional peal of thunder. Frieda was up in the cottage alone, and she got scared. She ran down to the farm and knocked loudly at the door, shouting, "Lorenzo, Lorenzo, where are you? Why do you leave me alone on such a night as this?" So Lawrence packed up his books and went home with her.

Q: Did Lawrence talk much about Frieda?

HOCKING: No. But sometimes when he was down at the farm and it was half past ten or more in the evening, he would say: "I think it's time we stopped our lesson now, Stanley. I must go up and see Frieda. She doesn't like being left alone so much."

Q: How did Lawrence happen to give you French lessons?

HOCKING: He was rather interested in me, and thought it a pity that I had left school at fourteen. He said: "You could have done

61

better, my boy." I told him it wasn't a question of going out into the world and looking for a job. My job was waiting for me on the farm, and there was always something to do. We had lots of cattle and sheep to look after in those days. So Lawrence offered to teach me French.

Q: Was he a good teacher?

Hocking: Oh yes. And very patient. Just before he left Tregerthen, I remember him telling me: "I think you are a very good pupil, Stanley." He would give me little lessons, and he was always telling me that certain words in English did not translate.

Q: Lawrence knew French well?

HOCKING: He could speak French and Italian and German. A few days after the Spanish steamer *Manu* was wrecked in our cove, some of the Spanish sailors came back to see their old ship. I remember my mother giving them tea, and Lawrence came down to have a chat with them. The sailors couldn't speak any English. Lawrence tried to talk to them in Spanish, the few words he knew, but he couldn't get much sense out of them. Then he tried them in French, and they all talked a bit. After the sailors had left, Lawrence said to us: "That's funny. Those fellows can talk a better French than Spanish!"

Q: Tell me, Mr. Hocking, did you people hire Lawrence to help with the harvest?

HOCKING: Of course we never hired him! He wouldn't condescend to become a farm laborer! But he always would say: "I want to be one of you. I want to labor in the fields and help you with the harvest. Like one of you." He loved coming down and doing what he could. I know he used to come and ask: "Well, what are we going to do today?"

Q: Did Lawrence know much about farming?

HOCKING: No, I don't think so. But there must have been some farmer up near his home that he helped a bit as a lad. Otherwise, he wouldn't have known how to make those peculiar knots when he tied the sheaves.

Q: Peculiar knots?

HOCKING: He would bind the sheaves as we would call the Midlands way. He had a different method of making the knot. Our sheaves had to stand quite a bit of handling, and we had to bind them in a certain manner. Very tightly and very efficiently. Now Lawrence would bind them all right—they were bound by straw. Just a little wisp of straw you would pull out with your hand and twist and tack under. But I must admit that his sheaves wouldn't stand much handling. In the winter the sheaves had to be pulled out from the rick and carried through the barn to feed the cattle. This meant several more handlings. And if those sheaves weren't done properly, they would all come adrift. So that is why we could always tell at a glance: "Oh, this is one of Lawrence's sheaves here."

Q: What other things would he do that showed his inexperience on a farm?

HOCKING: Well, in pitching hay or corn. He wouldn't handle the fork in the orthodox manner that we stout country farmers did. We would take the fork, plunge it in, and fling the hay or corn up. But Lawrence had the inclination to hold the fork more like a woman—sometimes he hardly knew which hand to put forward first. In pitching hay, you're either left- or right-handed; Lawrence would try to use the fork both ways.

Q: What was Lawrence's favorite work on the farm?

HOCKING: Definitely harvesting, because it was always done in beautiful weather. The sun was shining and it was warm and comfortable. Frieda would sometimes come down and help with the harvest. Lawrence and Frieda were delighted when my sisters brought out croust in the afternoon.

Q: Croust?

HOCKING: Croust. You wouldn't know what that is, would you?

Q: No.

HOCKING: It's a Cornish word. I don't think you'll find it in the Oxford dictionary. I suppose the spelling would be c-r-o-w-s-t. It means tea served out of doors in the afternoon.

Q: Lawrence wrote in "The Nightmare" chapter of *Kangaroo* that he had almost left off writing and spent most of his time working in the fields.

HOCKING: Lawrence was writing, I know. If he was helping us in the fields and something occurred to him, he would drop what he was doing immediately, and go in and write for the next two or three hours. He had a typewriter, and after he had left a nearby field, we would sometimes hear the typewriter tapping away.

Q: Did Lawrence ever mention the Midlands farmer whom he worked for when he was a young man?

HOCKING: Not by name. He once said there was a farmer in the

Midlands where he used to go and tie the sheaves.

Q: Would he sometimes stay all day in the fields?

HOCKING: Yes, providing the weather was suitable. But he always knew what to do if he got tired. He would make some excuse, pack up, and go up the lane. And if it was pouring rain, you wouldn't see him for a week.

Q: Was Lawrence physically capable of doing the more difficult jobs?

HOCKING: He wasn't very strong. He could do the little—what shall I say?—the insignificant jobs in the fields and on the rick. He could get on the rick and hand the hay from the pitcher to William Henry who was building the rick—he loved that. He could do that better than pitching off a load. It's no joke, pitching off a load of hay from a wagon: that's hard work. But as soon as hay is taken from a wagon and placed on a rick, the hay is loose. Lawrence could hand loose hay or sheaves to the builder. A boy of eleven can do that. I've pitched many a load to Lawrence.

Q: Lawrence wrote that he loved you people at the farm. He said you weren't educated, but he felt you had an endless curiosity about the world. "An endless interest."

HOCKING: So he said we were not educated, did he? That's a sharp one, isn't it. What does an education do for you? In those days, going to college wouldn't have been an advantage in getting a living out of the soil as a Cornish farmer. You've got to be brought up into it. You've got to know what each individual field is capable of growing, and what it takes for attention to make things grow. Otherwise, you would be a failure. And this knowledge comes to you only with years of experience.

Q: In *Kangaroo*, I read: "'Now do you think it's right, Mr. Somers?' [Mr. Lawrence].   The times that Somers heard that question, from the girls [Mabel and Mary], from Arthur [Stanley], from
John Thomas [William Henry]." You people asked him a lot of
questions?

HOCKING: I dare say we did. But I think we were happier in our
way of life by not having contact with the outside world.   The
outside world didn't make Lawrence happier than we were.   He
might have seen too much of the ways of the world—too much for
his own good.

Q: Lawrence wrote: "He worked out of doors all the time—and he
ceased to care inwardly—he began to drift away from himself. He
was very thick with John Thomas, and nearly always at the farm."

HOCKING: Oh yes.   Lawrence and William Henry used to talk
together for hours after I had gone to bed. Lawrence was no clock
watcher, and neither was William Henry. If Lawrence had been in
the fields helping with the harvest, he would come to supper that
night at the farm and stay talking with William Henry until half
past ten or midnight.

Q: And where was Frieda?

HOCKING: Frieda was alone in the cottage: she rather liked his
going out in the daytime, as it gave her more freedom when he
wasn't around all the time. On fine days Lawrence would be out
helping us or tending his garden. This arrangement was quite suitable for Frieda. But she didn't like being left alone in the evening.

Q: And she was left alone a lot?

HOCKING: I must admit she was. Two or three evenings a week

Lawrence would come down to give me my French lesson. Then perhaps the following week I would go up there a couple of evenings. But if the weather was suitable, he would be down at the farm during the day. When it's raining you can't do anything important, except maybe cut weeds or clean out barns. It's only when the weather is fine that you can make hay.

Q: Lawrence was at ease in your home?

HOCKING: Oh yes, he used to sit in the kitchen. There was a big table a dozen people could sit around. The dresser was on the right side and there was a little seat by the old Cornish slab. Lawrence was very fond of sitting on this little seat, especially when mother was frying potatoes. As soon as the potatoes were ready, he'd be picking them out from the pan, one or two at a time, little potato slices, and putting them in his mouth, saying: "These are lovely, Mrs. Hocking! You are the best cook in the whole world!" Poor old Lawrence, I can see him doing that now.

Q: So Lawrence liked your mother's cooking?

HOCKING: Very much. Mother would often cook a joint of beef or a small chicken for them on Sundays. This used to please them. In those days, there was only a small oil stove for a cooking arrangement in the cottage—there wasn't a slab or range. If you had a Cornish slab, there would be an oven at the side, but with their oil stove the Lawrences had only a flame, and you had to watch it. If the flame got too high, the stove would smoke.

Q: Did you people feel that Frieda was different—perhaps more difficult to know than Lawrence?

HOCKING: She couldn't be considered one of us the way Lawrence was, and we had to admit she lived in a separate world from

67

us.

Q: And this made a difference?

HOCKING: A German baroness is not going to consider herself on the same level as an ordinary Cornish farm girl or wife. And her father was a German baron.

Q: And Lawrence?

HOCKING: Surely a Cornish farmer is as good as the son of a Nottinghamshire miner? And his father was only a Nottinghamshire miner.

Q: But Frieda *was* different?

HOCKING: There will always be that barrier. Call it a social barrier if you will, but it will always be there. Mind you, Frieda might have felt quite a bit isolated. She was a stranger in a strange land, and there was no one of her class in the locality for her to be friendly with. But Frieda wasn't class-conscious. Not as much as we were. Particularly, my mother and sisters—they felt the difference, I know. Women have a natural aptitude for feeling this sort of thing. I can remember one of my sisters saying: "She's more of a lady than he is." We loved for Frieda to come down in the fields, but my sisters were a bit uneasy—they had the feeling that Mrs. Lawrence was a lady.

Q: Lawrence believed that his working on the farm had a charm for Frieda. This aspect of him. "Careless, rather reckless in old clothes and an old battered hat."

HOCKING: Yes. I remember one day he was looking particularly ragged and sweaty. I heard Frieda say to Mother: "Lorenzo looks more like one of you every day. I don't know what I'm going to do with him!"

Q: Lawrence's battered appearance pleased Frieda?

HOCKING: I think Frieda was delighted that Lawrence had something rather definite to do. Apart from writing. You see, I think he considered that writing was going to be his future livelihood. He wasn't selling his work much then, so he turned his hand to things he could do. Such as helping us on the farm and growing his own vegetables.

Q: Lawrence claimed that the neighbors were jealous because he helped you people at the farm. In *Kangaroo,* Lawrence wrote that "work went like steam" when he gave you people a hand in the fields.

HOCKING: That's a good one! We had another workman and Lawrence was only considered a boy compared to him. Work "went like steam" not because of Lawrence—there were many days when he wasn't there, and work went on as usual. Now look here, this reminds me of a rather amusing remark that this other workman made about Frieda and Lawrence. This fellow was a bit of a lad and he had a droll wit. I remember we all had our tea in the fields at harvest one day, and after Frieda and Lawrence had gone home, this old boy said to me and William Henry: "Where in the hell did she find him? I should think that she must have found him in a Lucky Bag!"

Q: Lucky Bag?

HOCKING: In those days we could go to a shop and buy a half-penny Lucky Bag—a little bag made up and containing two or three sweets and maybe a thimble or a squeaker. You see, Lawrence felt that Frieda was superior to him. She had a different manner and she talked very nicely.

Q: What would she talk about?

HOCKING: She didn't talk about much. She didn't come in and sit down the way Lawrence did in the evening. When she came for the milk you could guess that Lawrence was rather unwell, and she would go back to give him his supper.

Q: Did Lawrence speak of his family when he was in the fields helping you people with the harvest?

HOCKING: I never heard him say anything about his background or his mother and father. He may have told William Henry a lot more than he told me. William Henry and Lawrence were more of an age—I was only a boy of sixteen.

Q: What did you have for livestock on Tregerthen farm?

HOCKING: A bit of everything: cattle, horses, sheep, pigs.

Q: Did he do much shearing?

HOCKING: Oh no! He wasn't strong enough to hold a sheep. It takes a bit of brute strength to hold one of our Oxford sheep that would probably weigh one hundred and fifty to one hundred and eighty pounds.

Q: Did Lawrence like animals?

HOCKING: Yes. And he was very fond of Blossom, our big cart horse. Blossom stood about seventeen hands high and weighed about a ton, and he used to ride her around the fields in his spare time. Lawrence always had a turn for things, and I remember he would say: "Gee-up, gee-up, my beautiful Blossom, you are my moving mountain!" And off they would go.

Q: In *Kangaroo*, Lawrence wrote that the neighbors hated him for his intimacy with you people. He said that each farm was bitterly jealous of the other.

HOCKING: I believe Lawrence was jumping to conclusions. We were all friends on the farms in those days, and I don't think our neighbors were interested at all in how friendly we were with the Lawrences. After all, Lawrence's cottage was only one little item in the countryside. People did not visit because everybody had more work to do during the war years. We had to plow and to plant about three times the ordinary acreage. People in Zennor village did gossip, but not on the farms. I think Lawrence invented this. He was very sensitive, and might have imagined that the entire parish was against him.

Q: With no fixed income, how did the Lawrences manage to provide for themselves.

HOCKING: This was a rather difficult time for them. Lawrence told us they had no money. He couldn't make much out of his writings, and Frieda had to depend on any money she got from Germany by way of Switzerland. We were given to understand that she got very little. But life was pretty simple in those days. They got their chief necessities of life at the farm from Mother. They could have butter, milk and eggs, an occasional chicken or rabbit. That would keep them from starving, and of course they always had a little money for groceries at the village shop or in St. Ives: bread, jam, cheese. Then too, Lawrence grew his own vegetables.

Q: Did he have a large garden?

HOCKING: Actually, he had two gardens. He had quite a respectable patch in one of our potato fields, and another enclosed garden closer to his cottage. This wasn't bigger than an average-sized room. We had planted this little patch for generations. Mother called it her rhubarb garden. My older brothers used to plant several crowns of rhubarb there and cover them carefully during the winter with an old can that had the bottom knocked out. The rhubarb crowns had died out and the garden was empty. We told Lawrence he could use this patch. When he wasn't busy writing or helping us in the fields, he would be planting and growing things. Carrots, parsnips, peas, lettuce, parsley, and what he was most fond of: spinach and endive.

Q: Lawrence mentioned in one of his letters that he had been cutting blackthorn and gorse all one day to make a fence in order to keep *your* lambs out of his garden.

HOCKING: I can't see how that could be. As soon as the lambs were old enough to climb fences we moved them to the fields up the road by Eagle's Nest.

Q: He must have had some trouble with lambs in his garden. He wrote S. S. Koteliansky on May 11, 1917, saying: "I loathe lambs, those symbols of Christian meekness. They are the stupidest, most persistent, greediest little beasts in the whole animal kingdom. Really, I suspect Jesus of having had *very little* to do with sheep, that he could call himself the lamb of God. I would truly rather be the little pig of God, little pigs are infinitely gayer and more delicate in soul."

HOCKING: He could make rather snippy remarks at just about anything. I recall we were watching the lambs play in front of his window. Mind you, he used to be interested and really amused in seeing them gamboling and playing on the tops of big rocks in the field and having races together. He used to like that. He said to me while we were watching them: "It's all very well to see the dear little lambs playing and gamboling, but what are they born for? Only for the cruel butcher's knife. Futile it all is," he said. "Every birth means a death. Therefore all life is futile."

Q: Did Frieda enjoy working in the garden?

HOCKING: Frieda wasn't the philosopher he was. She was gayer and liked to see the funny side of life.

Q: How so?

HOCKING: I know one day she said to me, while looking at the old sow: "I'm sure you farmers must make a fortune. Take one of your old sows, for instance. She has dozens and dozens of little pigs every year." It was so funny hearing these people make their little remarks.

Catherine Carswell (1914)

Lawrence and Frieda (1918)

The Tower cottage

Tregerthen farm

SUSPICION AND SURVEILLANCE

Q: In a letter to Middleton Murry, May 5, 1917, Lawrence wrote: "All the Cornish farmers are filled with the sense of inevitable disaster: talk freely of the end of the world." Did you expect a German invasion?

HOCKING: There was a genuine fear of being invaded, or perhaps being shelled out of existence. We were told that the Germans had millions of everything, and they could easily put more men into the field than we could. To offset this opinion, I heard the old men talking: "No, boy, they'll never land in this country. They'll never get this country. What do you think our navy would be doing if they tried to land here?" These were the general comforting statements being made. Shall I tell you an amusing story that goes against the Americans a bit?

Q: Please do.

HOCKING: In those days we had several American submarine chasers based at Penzance, and quite a lot of the Americans came ashore for a pint at the local hotel—this was towards the end of 1917. The beer was duly poured out by a rather attractive barmaid. One of the Americans took a sip, and said: "Say Miss, this goddamn beer tastes flat!" And the barmaid replied: "No wonder, my boy. It's been over here three years waiting for you to come!" The general feeling was that America should have entered the war long before she did. If Germany had beaten England, America would have been in trouble.

Q: Why were so many ships sunk off the five-mile strip of coast between Zennor and St. Ives?

HOCKING: It so happened that the ships were going up the Bristol Channel in convoys. I recall seeing them—maybe thirty or forty of them at a time. They would hug the coast until they got near St. Ives, then veer off to the northwest to avoid the rocky cliffs. The coastline from Land's End to St. Ives was a very suitable place for submarines to attack. The Germans knew the merchant ships would be passing there.

Q: If the Germans had invaded England, where do you think they would have established their beachheads?

HOCKING: A lot of people started thinking that the Germans would do it very quietly and secretly by submarine on our Cornish beaches. Probably send little raiding bands ashore, just to knock the wind out of us and to terrify us. Then people began thinking: What's to stop those fellows on a quiet night from running ashore in one of our nice little coves? They could come up to the farms and cut our throats. It was possible.

Q: And the Germans were winning in 1916.

HOCKING: They were winning in late 1916. There was no radio then, but we could see from our daily newspapers that the front was shifting. And there was the horrible list of casualties in the newspaper—it was terrifying: thousands of young men listed as killed or wounded. Some of them were young men we knew.

Q: Was there more activity off the Cornish coast in 1917 than in 1916?

HOCKING: Things were getting to be very difficult by 1917. In early 1916, up there in the country, one scarcely knew there was a war going on—we were far away from it all. We became scared in late 1916 and all of 1917. What aroused suspicion was that Lawrence moved into Higher Tregerthen, and gradually the submarines began sinking our ships.

Q: I understand that when the news came that Asquith was out of the British government and Lloyd George was in, this was a crisis for Lawrence?

HOCKING: I remember that. Lawrence said: "This is the end of my England as I know it." He didn't like Lloyd George. Why, I don't know. He referred to him as "a dirty little Welch toad." He said Lloyd George wasn't fit for office.

Q: Lawrence claimed that he didn't hold himself in, and said what he thought about the war.

HOCKING: He didn't hold his tongue altogether, but I don't think he made any remarks so people would suspect him. He would talk openly only with William Henry and my dear old Uncle Henry— Mother's brother. But he didn't converse much with other people.

Q: How did Lawrence and Frieda feel about the war?

HOCKING: They didn't want it at all, of course. I should have told you that at the Christmas party, before we finished, the conversation touched upon a variety of subjects. Some of which—shall I say—had an international touch? The Americans, Robert Mountsier and Esther Andrews, thought America should join in the war against Germany. This made it very uncomfortable and difficult for Frieda. I remember Lawrence saying: "All wars are futile and useless. They are never caused by the ordinary people. They never want war. Wars are caused by blundering statesmen." And then Lawrence said to Mountsier: "What will you have? More destruction? More war?" Frieda said very little—for or against the war. But I remember one day she and Lawrence were helping us in the harvest field, and there was a game going on at sea. German submarines had been there. They had torpedoed some ships only a day or two before. Apparently, a German submarine had been spotted, and it was being hunted by destroyers and airships and patrol boats. There was a grand circle of them just about a mile offshore on this particular day in August 1917. I remember Frieda saying to me: "The fools are at it again! What a terrible thing war is! Why must we have wars? In that submarine may be some of the boys I played with as a child, and there they are being hunted to death!"

Frieda shared Lawrence's horror of the war, and her German background placed them in a difficult position. Though she had lived in Nottingham for a number of years with one English husband, and now in a wartime England with the second, her loyalties to Germany were strong. Frieda disliked the Kaiser, but she was proud that her younger sister, Johanna, had married Max Schreibershofen, aide-de-camp to the crown prince. Two von Richthofen cousins had joined the German Air Force, and both became leaders. One of these cousins was Manfred von Richthofen, the most famous of all German flyers during World War I, the Red Baron.

"I used to think war so glorious," Frieda wrote Edward Marsh[26] on September 13, 1914, "my father such a hero with his iron cross and his hand that a bullet had torn." But the glory was gone for her now, and she deplored the waste of lives. She told Marsh that he must not hate her native land. "We are frightfully nice people, but it is so difficult for the English to understand anything that is *not* English."

This was written at the beginning of the war, before a generation of men had been killed on the battlefields and hatred for anything

German had solidified at home. Frieda, with her tactlessness, taxed the patience of several of Lawrence's friends. Violet Hunt,[27] reader for Ford Madox Hueffer's (later Ford Madox Ford)[28] *English Review*, had known Lawrence when he was teaching in Croydon. Violet Hunt, in the company of Hueffer and Mrs. H. G. Wells, visited one day when Lawrence was away. During a conversation with Frieda, Hunt mentioned Hueffer's popular poem "Antwerp," a poem inspired by the sight of Belgian refugees at Charing Cross Station. "Dirty Belgians!" Frieda was reported to have said. "Who cares for them!" Hueffer claimed he went to an outhouse to escape Frieda's tirade of pro-Germanism because he was wearing the uniform of his country. Frieda, in a 1955 letter to Harry T. Moore, insisted there was no outhouse where they were living, that the visit occurred before Hueffer joined the forces, and denied ever having made such a remark about Belgians.

Frieda was often indiscreet in parading her Teutonic background before acquaintances and strangers. She would sing German songs, dress in her Bavarian costume, and proudly reveal her family's baronial connections. She was too outgoing to keep her divided sympathies to herself; too naive to realize that she was often the enemy in the eyes of those who were in her company. David Garnett, in his book, *Flowers of the Forest*, wrote that from the beginning of the war Frieda "found herself already being cold-shouldered and disliked because of her German origin." The Lawrences visited Garnett and one of his Imperial College friends at Garnett's flat and when they left the friend called down to Frieda "'Auf Wiedersehen Gnädige Baronin!' and Frieda called back gaily to us in German." The remark prompted the visits of several detectives who were suspicious of Garnett and his visitors. It was obviously not the time or place for German farewells.

Q: When did the local authorities begin to keep a watch on Lawrence's cottage for lights?

HOCKING: Things didn't come to a head all of a sudden—it took several months. Roughly speaking, from June to October. Very quietly, the police and the coast guards were keeping a watch on his cottage for lights at night. It was quite a while before we got to know about this. I'm sure that Lawrence never showed any lights to the sea—if he had, he would have been immediately prosecuted. Lawrence knew the blackout law was enforced. No lights were to be shown to the sea, and he kept to it.

Q: I understand Lawrence was warned by one of his Cornish friends that the coast watchers had very strict orders to keep an eye on him and his wife. Who was this friend?

HOCKING: William Henry.

Q: And when he was warned, Lawrence said that the authorities could go to hell.

HOCKING: I remember my brother telling this. When Lawrence knew that his own countrymen were suspecting him of being unfaithful and being a spy, he said: "What can you feel like? It drags me down into the dust."

Q: What were the reasons for people to suspect Lawrence and Frieda of spying for the Germans?

HOCKING: They didn't look like the ordinary people of West Cornwall. They were different. There was nobody in the locality who dressed the way Lawrence did, with his corduroy suit and slouch hat and beard and Victorian collar and tie. His collar and tie reminded me of old Gladstone. Then there was the submarine fear, submarines sinking our ships right in view of Lawrence's cottage. People very soon got to know that Frieda was German. They knew Lawrence was English enough, but of course, since he

was married to a German, they didn't know if his affections had remained English. And then the remark was being passed: "You
never know what these people are up to. They could have a secret
code for signalling to the German submarines and giving the position of our ships."

Q: Catherine Carswell claimed that Lawrence shouldn't have settled near the coast with a German wife in the first place. That he
should have moved inland before he was suspected of signalling to
the Germans.

HOCKING: I don't think that occurred to Lawrence. When he
came to Tregerthen, he was delighted with it. And why should he
live inland? He loved his little cottage, and he loved looking at
the sea. Besides, in early 1916, the war seemed far away there in
the country.

Q: Were you or any member of your family blamed for being
friendly with the Lawrences?

HOCKING: Yes, some people did say we were "being friendly
with those foreigners out there." But we had no reason to criticize
the Lawrences in any way. They were perfectly nice to us.

Q: I understand some neighbors were beginning to suspect your
brother too? Local people who had known William Henry all their
lives?

HOCKING: I believe a few did begin to suspect him. You see,
my brother and Lawrence were such jolly good friends.

Q: Did Lawrence say: "I am not a spy. I leave it to dirtier people.
I am myself and I won't have popular lies."

HOCKING: He did say that. And I remember him saying, when he knew he was being watched: "Fancy that. Thinking I am a spy. What is there to spy on here? In fact, I'm no more guilty of spying than the rabbits in the fields." Rabbits used to come out right in front of his back window, and Lawrence would watch them playing in the early morning.

Q: He claimed, in *Kangaroo*, that he was being spied on by men who lay behind the stone fences. "It is a job the Cornish loved," wrote Lawrence.

HOCKING: I don't think he should have referred to the authorities as Cornish. The coast guards were definitely not Cornish. Neither were the military. I'm doubtful if some of the police were even Cornish. And besides, Lawrence's cottage was only one item on the landscape.

Several people in Zennor who lived through this difficult time and who read "The Nightmare" chapter of *Kangaroo* resented Lawrence's opinion of the Cornish reaction to the war. "We weren't as bad as Lawrence said," replied an elderly customer over his pint at the Tinners Arms.

Giuseppe Orioli[29] thought otherwise. Orioli wrote in his autobiography, *Adventures of a Bookseller,* 1937, that he remembered "a nice old woman at Zennor" who stated she would like to hang the Kaiser and eat his heart—a woman who had lost no relatives in the war. Orioli also claimed that he knew a lecturer on Italian art who had given up his native German citizenship to become an English subject and had settled in Cornwall. But the Cornish began to suspect him of spying and he was watched and his cottage searched on several occasions. ("I never heard of such a thing!" declared Stanley Hocking.) The lecturer's heart was weak and he was unable to walk to nearby Penzance. When the Penzance merchants refused to deliver his groceries, two sympathetic girls brought his food to him. One day the police found a note he had written for the girls, and the authorities decided that the word *macaroons* was a code word for the gasoline which he was suspected of supplying to German submarines. "From that day onward he was tortured" by the police and his neighbors "into such a state of depression and misery that he killed himself."

In *Musical Chairs*, Cecil Gray admitted that "there was just a shred of justification for the distrust and suspicion which Lawrence had aroused in official circles, apart from his German wife, his reputation as a writer of immoral tendencies, and the unfortunate episode in which we had been involved together"—Gray meant the showing of the light at Bosigran when the Lawrences were visiting. The young musician felt that Lawrence was "indiscreet in speech when in company of people whom he may sometimes wrongly have supposed to be trustworthy." (Gray definitely meant the Hocking family—particularly William Henry.) More than once Lawrence revealed to Gray plans of "initiating a disruptive, pacifist and nihilist campaign in the industrial North, with a view to bringing about a speedy end to the War." Gray claimed that Lawrence was determined to embark upon such an adventure and when asked if he would accompany Lawrence, Gray "agreed unhesitantly" to the plan, for "such was the extent of his influence over me in these days."

Gray believed that some of Lawrence's long talks were overheard by the authorities. "One of the less engaging aspects of the Cornish character consists in a mania for spying and listening at keyholes or windows." Gray was certain that both he and Lawrence were under surveillance. Nothing ever came of Lawrence's plan to disrupt the industrial apparatus of England—"it was all talk," wrote Gray, "mere hot air," but some of Lawrence's wilder discourse could have been relayed to military headquarters. Cecil Gray felt that the times "only required a leader with a sense of direction to render" such disruptive plans and Lawrence was "potentially such a leader." Then Gray suggested: "He was, indeed, the stuff of which Hitlers are made, especially at that time when his great gifts were unrecognized and he was on the verge of penury."

Q: In *Kangaroo,* I find: "It was not till afterwards that he learned that the watchers had lain behind the stone fence to hear what he and Harriet [Frieda] had talked about." Is this so?

HOCKING: I can show you the very place—in front of the north window which overlooked one of our fields.

Q: These watchers were behind a fence?

HOCKING: Not exactly behind a fence. Lawrence would put it that way. There was no fence in front of his back window because our field was there. If he liked, he could have jumped out of his back window straight into the field. Those fellows could have been there in the dark without Lawrence knowing it, and I firmly believe they were. But he wouldn't have any occasion to go out there much after dark.

Q: Were those watchers seen at any time?

HOCKING: I didn't actually see them. But we heard from an indirect channel that they were there. Probably William Henry knew they were keeping a watch. I imagine it would have been difficult to hear any conversation from the ocean side of the cottage. They definitely couldn't wait in front because it was a public lane leading down to the farm, and if Lawrence or Frieda had opened the door the watchers would have been immediately detected.

Q: When the chimney of Lawrence's cottage was tarred, the local people said it was some signal to the German submarine crews. Do you remember any of this?

HOCKING: I remember the chimney being done. But that remark is all nonsense. I don't know who could have started that rumor.

Q: Some people thought Lawrence and Frieda were carrying food to the German submarine crews.

HOCKING: That too is sheer nonsense. By golly, everything was rationed! You could scarcely get enough food to satisfy yourself, let alone carry food to the Germans.

Q: It was rumored that the Lawrences had a secret store of petrol hidden in the cliffs.

HOCKING: I can guess how these silly remarks came into being. During those war years with so many ships being torpedoed, all sorts of articles were being washed ashore. Bales of hay, cases of matches, slabs of candle grease; I can truthfully say I came across these myself. They weren't worth much. And yes, some tins of petrol were being washed ashore—this was in 1917. The petrol had probably been in a steamer that was torpedoed on its way to France. The tins had been smashed about and were leaking, and you could smell petrol when you went down by the cliffs on certain days. That must have started this particular rumor.

Q: I understand that Frieda couldn't hang out a towel or empty the slops without being watched.

HOCKING: That's getting a bit thick. Men couldn't be on permanent watch for the Lawrences alone. There were miles of coast to cover.

Q: In *Not I, But the Wind,* Frieda writes of running and jumping with a white scarf blowing in the wind, and Lawrence telling her to stop before people would think that she was signalling the Germans.

HOCKING: That little incident happened one day while they were down by the cliffs. They used to frequently stroll over there. It's a marvelous view of Wicca Pool from the top of the cliff on the right, and Zennor Head can be seen on the left.

Q: I believe the authorities searched a bag of groceries that Frieda was carrying home from the store in Zennor.

HOCKING: Frieda met two coast watchers on the footpath, and they immediately stopped her. They wanted to know if she had a camera in her shopping bag. One wasn't allowed to take photographs in those days. In fact, I didn't get my camera until several years after the war—just to be safe. Frieda said she didn't have a camera and showed them the parcel. It was a loaf of bread. She said they looked mighty crestfallen.

Shortly before the Lawrences were ordered out of Cornwall, they visited Cecil Gray on a night when the wind was blowing a gale. The three sat before the fire and amused themselves by singing German folk songs. Suddenly, there was a hammering on the door, and as Gray rose from his chair the door was flung open. Several men with rifles entered and began to search the house. A light had been seen coming from a window. Gray explained that he had no knowledge of the light. What had happened was that the wind had blown loose one of the pins that held the curtain in place. A flicker of light had escaped at irregular intervals like a signal. "Finding nothing incriminating on the premises," wrote Gray, "the intruders withdrew, with operatic gestures like a Verdi chorus, and blood-curdling threats to the effect that I would hear more of the matter."

A few days later Gray was summoned to appear in court. It was more serious than he had realized. A German submarine had been reported in the vicinity of Gunard's Head at the moment the flickering light had been noticed. This, in addition to the singing of German folk songs with his German friend and her husband, placed Gray in an unpleasant situation.

Q: Lawrence had written that Frieda was continually frightened during the last months of their stay in Cornwall.

HOCKING: Yes, I do recall her getting nervous, and we must remember that she was German. Frieda had to be very careful. She wouldn't talk about the war with anyone in the village or St. Ives, and she worried about her friends and relations in Germany. One didn't know what was going to happen then. I think she was rather close with her family in Germany.

Q: Lawrence wrote that the authorities hated Frieda—"her reckless pride, her touch of derision."

HOCKING: It could be. But I never was present when any of the authorities interviewed the Lawrences. The officials would always pop up suddenly without any warning.

Q: Did you know Cecil Gray?

HOCKING: Not very well. He was living in the Bosigran Castle house which was on the very edge of the cliffs, out beyond Gunard's Head and two miles from the Lawrences. Gray's windows were all facing the sea. He was a stranger like Lawrence, and coming amongst us, a bit of suspicion fell on Gray too.

Q: I believe Gray showed a light?

HOCKING: Yes. Accidentally. Lawrence and Frieda were over there for an evening's visit when the incident occurred. The coast guards spotted the light, and Gray was summoned and fined twenty-five pounds.

Q: Some of Lawrence's literary friends have written that the policemen were all local people. No military authorities were mentioned, only the police and the coast watchers.

HOCKING: The military came in as an overlord to the police. The only military man directly concerned with the Lawrences was a major—I never knew his name. He was in charge of the Western Cornwall Division, and he was with the police when Lawrence was given notice to leave Cornwall.

Q: A person who is supposedly somewhat of an authority on that time in Cornwall said to me: "Don't you believe it. It was the people on those farms who suspected the Lawrences. The people would gossip, and they were suspicious of any strangers who came in their midst."

HOCKING: The few farmers and farmers' wives and the families close by didn't see the Lawrences enough to suspect and hate them. People didn't move around very much. Many would never have the occasion to see the Lawrences at all. Mind you, when the two would go into town, to say the least, they looked a bit outlandish. Nine times out of ten, Frieda would be wearing her bright-red stockings into St. Ives. And some would ask: "Well! Who are they?" Then the inevitable question: "Are they married?" I think some people worried more about this than the spy business.

Bosigran Castle

Zennor village

C. J. Stevens (left) and Stanley Hocking (1968)

Higher Tregerthen, Tregerthen farm and the sea

THE EXPULSION

Q: I understand the authorities broke into Lawrence's cottage and searched it while the two were away? Do you recall this incident?

HOCKING: The authorities could just walk in. Lawrence never locked any doors when he went out. Frieda came down to the farm and told us that the cottage had been searched. In short, the officials had left things in a hell of a mess. All of Lawrence's letters had been disturbed, and Frieda said that even her workbasket, where she kept her knitting things, had been torn apart and left on the floor. Lawrence told us that they couldn't have found anything because there was nothing for them to find. And the next day he was given notice to leave Cornwall within three days.

Q: In *Kangaroo,* I read that Frieda was at Cecil Gray's and Lawrence had gone to town with your brother and one of your sisters in the trap.

HOCKING: I don't recall that little detail, but it could be true. I do know that one of my sisters had seen two or three men going up the lane. They were in uniform. But we didn't know the cottage had been searched until Frieda came down and told us.

Q: The day he was given notice to leave, Lawrence claimed that you, "Arthur," the boy, had overheard one official say to the other as they went up the hill, after leaving the cottage: "Well, that's a job I would rather not have had to do."

HOCKING: Yes. I was by the roadside cutting some weeds when those fellows came by chatting. I wasn't supposed to hear this, but

I did.

In *Not I, But the Wind*, published in 1935, Frieda Lawrence wrote that there was a woman "even now who boasts that she turned us out of Cornwall as spies." Members of the Hocking family were reluctant to discuss this woman who hated the Lawrences, and a librarian at the St. Ives Library said to this author: "I am sure you have discovered many interesting things about D. H. Lawrence, but I would advise you to ignore whatever information you might have concerning the Vicar of Zennor and his daughter." When asked why this should be ignored the librarian's only explanation was "because it is very doubtful if this particular information would prove adequate for your purposes."

"Look here, this can be traced," said Stanley Hocking. "One can easily find out who the Vicar of Zennor was in 1916 and 1917. I've been warned about this little item. Both the vicar and his daughter are dead, but there are living relatives." The subject seemed to make Hocking most uncomfortable, but when asked why the vicar's daughter should boast that it was she who got the Lawrences out of Cornwall, he explained: "One of the chief agitators to get them out was the vicar. I don't know why entirely. But they never went to church. If you didn't go in those days, you were considered outside the circle of things. Frieda must have heard locally about this woman—possibly from some of their literary friends who were still around Cornwall from time to time after the war. And Lawrence knew a little about the vicar before they went away. I do remember the vicar asked me about the Lawrences: 'They are Germans, aren't they? What do you know about them?'"

"Lawrence got after me about the vicar and the church," said Stanley Hocking after pausing. "I was a lad in the choir then. He said to me: 'You go to church on Sunday. Don't you realize that you're singing a tremendous lot of lies?' I asked him how he made that out. 'You sing that you believe in the resurrection of the body and life everlasting, and any intelligent being knows that dead bodies do not rise again. It would be a terrible thing if they did! What would happen if all the graves were to open and the dead came trooping back? Wouldn't it be horrible? Their own friends and family wouldn't want to see them. What would we do with them?' I've got to admit that I was rather horrified—his pulling the story of the Bible to pieces."

Q: Do you think the authorities asked him to leave because they didn't want the bother of watching him?

HOCKING: That could be. They were on a wild-goose chase and they were watching him for nothing.

Q: How did Lawrence react to this three-day notice?

HOCKING: I remember him saying: "This is hateful. What have I done?" He loved his little cottage in Cornwall. He was perfectly happy here, war or no war, and he didn't have enough money to go travelling elsewhere. It all happened so suddenly.

Considering the expulsion from a military point of view, it is surprising that the order wasn't delivered earlier. The local police, coast watchers, and military have been criticized repeatedly for their conduct throughout the Cornish episode, and spokesmen of Lawrence's life have been quick to accuse the authorities of being insensitive and cruel. Were the two hounded, spied upon, and bullied for no reason at all? Lawrence and Frieda were strangers who moved to a coastal region just before submarine activity became alarmingly effective, Frieda was German, she was related to the Red Baron, Lawrence was the author of *The Prussian Officer and Other Stories*, his book *The Rainbow* had been reviewed as being unpatriotic, they both read German newspapers, they sang German songs, she sometimes proudly dressed in a German folk costume, he sometimes spoke and wrote of revolution and initiating disruptive campaigns, and they both were with Cecil Gray when the light was seen flickering.

Lawrence and Frieda never violated any of the restrictions imposed on civilians during the time in Cornwall and they minded their own business and willingly gave information when questioned. But they did arouse suspicion. Their presence was a nuisance to the authorities who had the responsibility of guarding miles of coast. It was easier to expel this couple than to waste valuable manpower. In a letter to Cecil Gray shortly after their arrival in London, Lawrence wrote: "We reported to police here—they had heard nothing about us, and were not in the least interested— couldn't quite see why we report at all. It is evident they work none too smoothly with the military."

But the London police soon became wary. A man from the Criminal Investigation Department was often seen watching the flat in Earl's Court where the Lawrences were staying, and on one visit Cecil Gray was rudely questioned by the official until Gray lost his temper and told the man to leave—the flat belonged to Gray's mother. Even after the Lawrences retreated to Dollie Radford's Berkshire cottage the surveillance continued, and a detective had gone to Ernest Weekley to see if the professor had any information to lodge against his former wife. If the injured ex-husband had been a revengeful person, he could have told the detective how Frieda once saw their son, Charles Montague Weekley, in an Officers' Training Corps uniform, and astonished the young man by saying: "Let me hide you somewhere in a cave or in a wood. I don't want you to go and fight. I don't want you to be killed in this stupid war."

Q: Lawrence has written that before he left Cornwall he made a great fire of all his old manuscripts.

HOCKING: Yes, he did. He was very upset by the turn of events.

Q: Do you remember the day the Lawrences left?

HOCKING: On the day they left, they came down to the farm to say good-bye. It was all in such a hurry. I remember my mother giving them some milk and sandwiches to take on the train because it was going to be a rather long journey. I'm not certain, but I believe that William Henry gave them a little money to help them along.

Q: Did Lawrence say he would be back?

HOCKING: He did say he would be back to see us all again. But he never did, poor fellow.

Q: Lawrence claimed that William Henry drove them to St. Ives in the trap, and you took the big luggage in the cart.

HOCKING: Yes. They couldn't take all their luggage in the market trap. The military officer and the police sergeant were there at the station to see that they got on the train. I remember that. The officials just stood there and said nothing. Nobody spoke. All these people are dead now.

Q: Did Lawrence occasionally write to you people after he left Cornwall?

HOCKING: Yes. He wrote William Henry several letters. But my brother would never answer a letter. He was no correspondent.

Lawrence's Cornish farmer loved to tell stories to his cronies on market day in Penzance, and more than once he had bragged about the man who wrote books and his wife who was a German baroness. But someone to whom he chatted had little sympathy for the bearded man and Germans. "William Henry said something about Frieda being German," recalled P.O. Eddy, "and the police came over to the farm and questioned him. I think the officers warned him that he could be locked up." The visit from the authorities worried the farmer, and though the friendship continued, William Henry was more careful when peddling butter and eggs in Penzance. In a letter to Robert Mountsier, December 9, 1920, Lawrence wrote: "Of Wm. Henry—he is married, with two little girls, prosperous in money—but household not happy—Mrs. Hocking ill and miserable. I don't hear from them direct. I think Wm. H. was scared when we were kicked out of Zennor and you were a 'Spy'."

William Henry kept a small diary, which is now in the hands of his son, H. H. Hocking. "Father started it in 1914," Hocking explained. "The diary is just notes that my father would refer to over a period of years to see what he had done on the fields. There is only one entry concerning Lawrence." When asked what the entry was, Hocking replied: "October 15, 1917. To St. Ives—Lawrence."

1. ASQUITH, LADY CYNTHIA, COUNTESS OF OXFORD AND ASQUITH (1885-1960). Met Lawrence in 1913. Born Cynthia Charteris, eldest daughter of Lord and Lady Wemyss. Married the Hon. Herbert Asquith in 1910. Secretary to Sir James M. Barrie (1918-1937). Corresponded frequently with Lawrence. Author of two volumes of autobiography: *Haply I May Remember* (1950) and *Remember and Be Glad* (1952). Editor of *The Ghost Book* (1926) and *The Black Cap* (1927).

2. THORNE, GUY, pseudonym of CYRIL ARTHUR EDWARD RANGER GULL (1876-1923). Journalist and prolific novelist. Author of *Miss Malevolent* (1899), *From the Book Beautiful* (1900), *Back to Lilacland* (1901), etc. Lawrence wrote Katherine Mansfield on March 8, 1916: "There are lovely stories to hear, about Guy Thorne, alias Ranger Gull, and these cottages. His silk-hat box, mouldy after two years of neglect, hangs in your pantry— and that is all there is of him, save the black and white panels, and orange roof, of your tower room. These black and white panels must be hushed up before you come."

3. MURRY, JOHN MIDDLETON (1889-1957). Author, editor, and critic. He and Katherine Mansfield met the Lawrences in 1913. Married Mansfield in 1918. On staff of *Westminster Gazette* (1912-1913) and art critic for that publication (1913-1914). Reviewer for *Times Literary Supplement* (1914-1918). Served in Political Intelligence Dept. of War Office (1916-1919). Editor of *Athenaeum* (1919-1921), of *Adelphi* (1923-1930), and of *Peace News* (1940-1946). Author of *Son of Woman* (1931, 1954), *Reminiscences of D. H. Lawrence* (1933), and the autobiography *Between Two Worlds* (1934).

4.   MANSFIELD, KATHERINE, pseudonym of KATHLEEN BEAUCHAMP (1888-1923). Short story writer. She and Middleton Murry were witnesses at the marriage of Lawrence and Frieda (July 1914). Born in Wellington, New Zealand. Married George Bowden (1909), John Middleton Murry (1918). From 1918 sought health in Italy, Switzerland, France. Died of tuberculosis at Fontainebleau, France.

5.   KOTELIANSKY, SAMUEL SOLOMNOVICH. Ukranian translator. Moved to England in 1914 and met Lawrence that summer. With Lawrence, Katherine Mansfield, Virginia Woolf, Leonard Woolf, he collaborated in translating works of Tolstoi, Dostoyevsky, Chekhov, Gorky, Bunin, etc. "Kot," as he was known, was the man to whom Lawrence wrote more frequently than to any other person. Koteliansky had come to England on a scholarship from the University of Kiev to do research in economics. He had been under suspicion in his own country for his radical views and had elected to stay on in England. Koteliansky liked Lawrence immensely, but the swarthy Russian with the fiery black glances could never warm to Frieda. Nor she to him. In *Lorenzo in Taos*, Mabel Dodge Luhan revealed Frieda's feelings for Koteliansky. He was the enemy. Kot felt that she wasn't good enough for Lawrence; that she didn't do enough for her husband. Frieda claimed that Koteliansky wanted to separate them. "Everyone thinks Lawrence is so wonderful." Frieda reportedly told Mrs. Luhan. "Well, I'd like to see him (Kot) live with Lawrence a month—a week! He might be surprised."

"Koteliansky was by far Katherine's most understandable friend," recalled Middleton Murry. There was more than friendship involved here and Murry was aware of it. He knew about Mansfield's destructive sexual encounters, her lesbianism, and her frequent affairs with men, but Murry preferred to overlook these adventures. Though, as a couple, they were able to survive numerous disasters, many of Katherine's friends felt that Murry was afraid of life and lacked the vitality to make his and Mansfield's relationship a success. From the beginning of their marriage Katherine took the dominant role, and he comfortably became the submissive partner. The Lawrences' sympathies were with Murry while Koteliansky stood by Katherine—Koteliansky delighting in her escapades.

6. CARSWELL, CATHERINE, nee CATHERINE ROXBURGH MACFARLANE (1879-1946). Scottish author. Met Lawrence in Summer 1914 and became devoted friend. Married Herbert Jackson (1903), Donald Carswell (1915). Drama critic and reviewer for *Glasgow Herald* (1907-1911). Author of the novels *Open the Door* (1920) and *The Camomile* (1922). Other books include *The Life of Robert Burns* (1930), and *The Savage Pilgrimage* (1932, 1951).

Catherine Carswell visited the Lawrences in 1916. It was her first stay with them and proved to be an agreeable one. Carswell, who had mostly praise for Lawrence, was not the kind to arouse Frieda's jealousy. There was an impersonality in her relations with him and she made no emotional demands. Carswell, who was to be one of Lawrence's most faithful defenders, received more than 170 letters from him and their correspondence continued until a few months before his death.

During her visit, she aroused Lawrence's puritanical wrath. Carswell had retired to the tower cottage, and after undressing for bed she remembered a book she had left in the living room of the Lawrences' cottage where they were still up. "I had brought no dressing-gown with me, but there seemed to me no impropriety in my costume—an ankle-length petticoat topped by a long-sleeved woolen vest! Lawrence, however, rebuked me. He disapproved, he said, of people appearing in their underclothes."

In her book, *The Savage Pilgrimage*, Catherine Carswell carried further Lawrence's distaste for things he thought indecent. Carswell mentioned his hatred for the dog because of its public habits.

In such matters Lawrence was no advocate of the natural. Nor was he an apostle of the nude. "I am sure," she wrote, "that he put down all our civilized indecencies—our coquetries as well as our prurience—to a departure from natural reticence." Carswell admitted that it might seem strange to all who had not considered the matter carefully, but she was convinced that only a man like Lawrence could have written *Lady Chatterley's Lover.*

Catherine Carswell and the Lawrences did the daily chores in their respective cottages without outside help, and the houseguest was delighted when Lawrence told her that she adapted better to the ways of cottage life than most of their friends in London. Carswell noticed that when Lawrence wasn't writing he would be working at something else with the same intensity he gave his literary pursuits. "Once he bought a gauze shawl of Paisley pattern for Frieda—cheaply, because it had a moth in it—and set himself to make it whole without delay by mending it himself. It took him two entire days, working well into the night, and allowing only the shortest intervals for his meals." Carswell never saw Lawrence idle. He wasn't haunted by time or tortured by feelings of guilt; he seemed to work freely, eagerly and steadily until the task at hand was completed. She felt he had a tremendous capacity for enjoyment and work, and it wasn't in his character to harbor regrets and doubts. One day Lawrence might announce that he would never write another word, but this wasn't said in despair. It was more that he believed his life to be greater than his books. Then a week later he would send out a new manuscript of poems or mention that he was typing the beginning of a new novel. Frequently, he burned stacks of manuscripts, and once at Higher Tregerthen he nearly set the chimney on fire and worried the Hockings. There would always be a new thing to be written or some chore he could begin happily.

7.   PATMORE, BRIGIT. Briefly outlined her life in a letter to Edward Nehls, who was editing *D. H. Lawrence: A Composite Bio-*

graphy (1957): "Brigit Patmore was born in Ireland but has lived all her life in England or abroad. A novel, *No Tomorrow* (1929), has been published in America and a book of short stories, *This Impassioned Onlooker* (1926) in England; also two translations: *Marmontel's Memoirs*, and Constantin de Grunwald's *Nicholas I.* After marrying a grandson of Coventry Patmore, she became a friend of Violet Hunt and a constant frequenter of the circle of famous writers"—including Lawrence.

8. LUHAN (LUJAN), MABEL DODGE, nee MABEL GANSON (1879-1962). Autobiographer, hostess, patroness of arts, and a long-time resident of Taos, New Mexico. Encouraged Lawrence to come to New Mexico in 1922 for the purpose of writing about American Indian life. She married Antonio ("Tony") Luhan, Pueblo Indian, in 1923. Author of autobiography *Intimate Memories.* She is best known for her *Lorenzo in Taos* (1932).

9. UNTERMEYER, LOUIS (1885-1977). American poet, editor, anthologist. *Moses* (1928) he considers the "best of his fiction... a combination of historical reconstruction and poetic fantasia." His marriage to Jean Starr Untermeyer (1907) was dissolved. He first met Lawrence in Italy and later the two saw each other in London (1926). Lawrence draws this picture of Untermeyer in a letter to Mabel Dodge Luhan (September 23, 1926): "I have seen a few of the old people: and yesterday the Louis Untermeyers: extraordinary, the ewige Jude, by virtue of not having a real core to him, he is eternal. Plus ça change, plus c'est la même chose: that is the whole history of the Jew, from Moses to Untermeyer: and all by virtue of having a little pebble at the middle of him, instead of an alive core."

10. WEEKLEY, ERNEST (1865-1954). Etymologist. Educated at universities in England, Switzerland, France, and Germany. Married Frieda von Richthofen (1899). There were three children:

Charles Montague, Elsa, and Barbara. Marriage dissolved (1914). During his forty years at the University of Nottingham, he served as Professor of French, Head of Dept. of Modern Languages, Dean of the Faculty of Arts. Author of many papers and books on the English language, including *The Romance of Words* (1912), *Words Ancient and Modern* (1926), and several etymological dictionaries.

11. GARNETT, DAVID (1892-1981). English writer. Met Lawrence in 1912. Son of Edward and Constance Black Garnett. Educated as biologist at Imperial College of Science. Partner of Francis Meynell in Nonesuch Press (1923-1935). Director of Rupert Hart-Davis, Ltd. Author of many novels from *Lady into Fox* (1922) to *Aspects of Love* (1955). His autobiographical works include *The Golden Echo* (1953) and *The Flowers of the Forest* (1955).

12. GRAY, CECIL (1895-1951). Scottish composer and author. After the Cornish episode, Lawrence and Frieda stayed at the flat of Gray's mother. Edited *The Sackbut*, a critical journal, with Philip Heseltine. Music critic for the *Nation* and *Athenaeum* (1925-1930); on staff of *Daily Telegraph* (1928-1932); music critic for *Manchester Guardian* (1931-1932). His three operas were *Deirdre, The Temptation of St. Anthony,* and *The Trojan Women.* Wrote biography of Philip Heseltine, *Peter Warlock* (1934). His autobiography was *Musical Chairs* (1948).

When Cecil Gray came down from London, Lawrence happily saw him installed at Bosigran. "Our friendship ripened quickly," Gray noted in *Musical Chairs*, "and within a very short time we used to meet virtually every day, either at his place or at mine, over a period of many months." A friendship did ripen, but during those four and a half months in Cornwall from early July to mid-October, when both men were neighbors, Lawrence often had other priorities. When the days were sunny, Lawrence felt that William Henry required him in the fields. "I feel pledged to help with the hay while the weather lasts," Lawrence wrote Gray, "so will postpone coming to Bosigran for a day or two."

The friendship between Gray and Lawrence didn't survive for long—there were too many complications—and it never reached the intensity of a Middleton Murry or William Henry relationship. As early as the spring of 1918, the union was all but over. Lawrence later asked Gray to run errands for him, such as packing the belongings left at Higher Tregerthen, but Lawrence couldn't conceal his irritation. On March 12, 1918, he wrote Gray: "I don't know why you and I don't get on very well when we are together. But it seems we don't. It seems we are best apart." Gray felt that Lawrence expected his friends to give up their personalities if friendship was to survive. To surrender completely. But Catherine Carswell named Gray as one of those who failed Lawrence. Carswell felt that Gray didn't give him "the responsive friendship that he craved and deserved." Gray denied this and claimed that he assisted Lawrence during the difficult time when the military authorities expelled her hero from Cornwall and the only thanks he got in return was "to be pilloried and caricatured" in two of Lawrence's books. "Apart from the chapter alluded to in *Kangaroo*, (The Nightmare) which is more or less accurate *reportage* and merely represents me as a faintly unpleasant nonentity (James Sharpe), I am portrayed in *Aaron's Rod* under the guise of a musician called Cyril Scott." Gray believed if the composer who did bear that name had brought a libel action against Lawrence, the real Cyril Scott would have been "awarded substantial damages, for a more nauseating specimen of the human race could hardly be imagined."

Gray made himself useful at the time of the expulsion by giving the Lawrences money and writing his mother to arrange for them to stay in her vacant London flat at Earl's Court. But he soon felt that he was being used by Lawrence and that too much was expected of him. More than he realized. Shortly after Lawrence's arrival in London, in a letter to Catherine Carswell, a new Rananim crew was named. They would all settle on a slope in the Andes. "Gray can find £1000." The musician was astonished to learn that he had been appointed to finance the expedition. His parents had money, but his allowance was only two hundred pounds a year. He now had little interest in Rananim, though he had agreed to such an adventure earlier. The thought of spending the rest of his life in the Andes with Lawrence, Frieda, William Henry, the Carswells, Koteliansky, and others wasn't Gray's idea of paradise.

13. HOBSON, HAROLD. Friend of David Garnett. Met Lawrence and Frieda on the high road from Germany to Italy with Garnett in 1912.

14. RAVAGLI, CAPT. ANGELO. B. 1891. Third husband of Frieda. Born in Tredozio, Italy. Saw service in World War I. Met the Lawrences in 1925. In 1933, came with Frieda to New Mexico to help her on Kiowa Ranch, the Lawrences' property. Married Frieda (1950) and became an American citizen.

15. DELAVENAY, EMILE. Author of *D. H. Lawrence: The Man and His Work, The Formative Years, 1885-1919* (1972), and *D. H. Lawrence and Edward Carpenter: A Study in Edwardian Transition* (1971). Delavenay retired as Professor of English at the University of Nice and was awarded *la Croix de Chevalier de la Légion d'Honneur* in 1972.

16. TRILLING, DIANA. B. 1905. American critic. Her largest literary impression was the column "Fiction in Review" in the *Nation* from 1941 to 1948. Her literary, political, and general cultural essays were published in such magazines as *Partisan Review, Commentary, Look,* and others. She edited and wrote the introduction for the 1961 edition of *Selected Letters of D. H. Lawrence.*

17. MINCHIN, MRS. CECILY, nee CECILY LAMBERT. With her cousin, Violet Monk (later Mrs. Violet Stevens), she took over Grimsbury Farm, Hermitage, Berkshire, during World War I. Friend of Lawrence and Frieda during their Hermitage stay (1918-1919).

18. ALDINGTON, RICHARD (1892-1962). English poet, biographer, novelist, critic, translator, and editor. Friend of Lawrence from 1914. Served in World War I (1916-1918). Author of *D. H. Lawrence: An Indiscretion* (1927); *Life for Life's Sake* (1941); *D. H. Lawrence: Portrait of a Genius, But...* (1950). He and Giuseppe Orioli edited Lawrence's *Last Poems* (1932).

19. MOUNTSIER, ROBERT (1888-1972). American journalist. Mountsier was Lawrence's literary agent in New York from 1916 to 1923.

20. ANDREWS, ESTHER. American journalist. In a letter to Catherine Carswell on December 26, 1916, Lawrence wrote: "Miss Andrews and Robert Mountsier have come up and are staying till the end of the week. They are very nice really. Yesterday we had a party with the Hockings, which was jolly. But my heart never felt so down in the dirt, as it does now."

21. LOW, BARBARA (1877-1955). She was an early Freudian psychoanalyst in England. Author of *Psycho-Analysis: A Brief Outline of the Freudian Theory* (1920).

22. MOORE, HARRY T. (1908-1981). American biographer and editor. He edited *The Collected Letters of D. H. Lawrence, D. H. Lawrence's Letters to Bertrand Russell, A D. H. Lawrence Miscellany,* and others. His books include *The Novels of John Steinbeck, The Life and Works of D. H. Lawrence,* and *The Intelligent Heart.* Moore was a frequent reviewer for *The New York*

Times, Saturday Review and other periodicals.

23. RADFORD, DOLLIE (1864-1920). English poet. She met Lawrence in 1915 and loaned him her cottage at Hermitage in 1918.

24. STARR, MEREDITH. Author of *The Future of the Novel* (1921). In this book Starr had nothing to say concerning the work of his neighbor, D. H. Lawrence.

25. STARR, LADY MARY. Lawrence described her in a letter to Lady Cynthia Asquith as "a half-cast daughter of the Earl of Stamford. They (the Starrs) fast or eat nettles: they descend naked into old mine-shafts, and there meditate for hours upon their own transcendent infinitude: they descend on us like a swarm of locusts and devour all the food on the shelf or board: they even gave a concert, and made the most dreadful fools of themselves in St. Ives: violent correspondence in *St Ives Times*."

William Henry's uncle, P. O. Eddy, clearly remembered Starr and Lady Mary. "The couple down at Treveal weren't Zennor people either. As youngsters, some of us would go down there and talk with them. I remember we went down one night, and we saw that they had big stones on their roof. Starr had covered his roof with a tarpaulin to keep the rain out and had put little stones on first, and the tarpaulin had stayed down for six weeks. 'Now I have larger stones on the roof,' he said. He didn't think of mending it! Things like this amused we Cornish people."

26. MARSH, SIR EDWARD (1872-1953). English writer and editor. Met Lawrence in 1913. Editor of *Georgian Poetry* (1912-1922). Private secretary to Winston Churchill (1905, 1917-1922, 1924-1929). Author of *Memoir of Rupert Brooke* (1915), *A Number of People* (1939), and *Minima* (1947), etc.

27. HUNT, VIOLET (1866-1942) English novelist and biographer. Reader for Ford Madox Ford on *English Review*. Met Lawrence when he was teaching at Croydon. Wrote for the *Pall Mall Gazette* and became an active worker for woman suffrage. Her autobiography, *I Have This to Say*, was published in 1926.

28. FORD, FORD MADOX (original surname Hueffer) (1873-1939). Founder of *English Review* (1908). First published Lawrence in 1909. During World War I he served as an officer in the Welsh Fusiliers. Later moved to France and was American Editor of *transatlantic review*. Among his best-known works is the tetralogy *Parade's End* (1924-1928).

29. ORIOLI, GIUSÈPPE (1884-1942). Italian bookseller and publisher. Met Lawrence in Cornwall. Supervised publication of *Lady Chatterley's Lover*. Published Lawrence's translation of *The Story of Doctor Manente, The Virgin and the Gipsy,* and *Apocalypse.*

Orioli could never warm to Lawrence. He found the fretful and distrustful part of Lawrence's personality too pronounced for a close relationship. Orioli objected to Lawrence's high opinion of his own work and to his feelings of not being sufficiently appreciated. "So far as such domestic arts were concerned he might have been a woman. He took more pride and pleasure in them than many women do; much more than his wife did." The Italian bookseller described his business relations with the author as being more difficult than any he had ever experienced. Real friendship was impossible.

INDEX

INDEX

ABOUT THE AUTHOR

C. J. Stevens is a native of Maine. His poems, stories, translations, and interviews have appeared in approximately five hundred publications and more than sixty anthologies and textbooks. He is the author of four collections of poetry: *Beginnings*, *Circling at the Chain's Length*, *Hang-Ups*, and *Selected Poems*; a previous biographical study on D. H. Lawrence, *Lawrence at Tregerthen*, was published in 1988; his other books are *The Next Bend in the River* and *Maine Mining Adventures* (history and adventure); *One Day With a Goat Herd* (animal behavior); and *The Folks from Greeley's Mill* (short stories). Stevens has traveled extensively and has lived in England, Ireland, Holland, Malta, and Portugal.